Exceptionality

Exceptionality

HOW TO BUILD A PERSONAL BRAND THAT'S WILDLY UNIQUE AND WORLD CLASS

Jane Anderson

Editing: Kristen Lowrey

Typeset by BookPOD

ISBN: 978-0-6485022-0-3 (pbk)
eISBN:978-0-6485022-1-0 (ebook)

NATIONAL
LIBRARY
OF AUSTRALIA

A catalogue record for this
book is available from the
National Library of Australia

To my parents, Don and Toni,
for always setting the standard.

About the author

Jane Anderson is a strategic communications expert and is passionate about working with women in consulting. She has over 20 years' experience in corporate communications and capabilities, and she has worked with over 100,000 people to elevate their influence in their businesses and careers.

Jane has recently been voted as one of the top three branding gurus globally. She has won more than 25 marketing, sales and communication awards and also has one of the top 1% most viewed LinkedIn profiles.

She is the host of the iTunes podcast *The Jane Anderson Show*, and has achieved acclaim interviewing thought leaders and experts such as Seth Godin. Jane has also been featured in *Business Insider*, *Sky Business*, the *Sydney Morning Herald* and *The Age*, and she is a contributor on *Forbes*.

Her clients include some of the world's leading experts in their field, as well as iconic brands such as Virgin Australia, Lego, Ikea, Rio Tinto and Origin Energy.

Jane is also dedicated to helping female consultants position and promote themselves, and ensure that they're charging what they're worth. She has built (and continues to build) a diverse group of like-minded female industry leaders who support and help each other grow their practices.

Obsessed with elevating influence in all areas, Jane is the author of nine books, speaks at conferences and delivers group and one-on-one mentoring to consultants looking to grow their practices. She lives in Brisbane, Australia with her husband Mark and stubborn English Bulldog, Winston.

Acknowledgements

In 2010 I was the head of capability for a large global multinational retailer. On a Saturday morning I went into the office to work on the design of a time management program. As I sat there to write it, I realised how ironic it was that I was working on a weekend to create a time management program. I felt like an absolute imposter.

So I called a colleague, friend and fellow coach Stacey Ashley and asked if she would coach me on how to become more productive. Thankfully she did and it was truly life changing. Whilst I like to think I'm a naturally organised person, I had never been taught some of the productivity tools that she taught me. And they had such an impact that I went on to work for the productivity company she worked for and this sparked my obsession with systems, continuous improvement and high performance.

Up until this time my obsession was with helping people to find their uniqueness in their personal brand as leaders and in their careers. I loved helping people to hone in on their strengths and to use them to really stand out and find flow in their work and lives.

So, when the opportunity came to learn about continuous improvement, I realised that it has so much to do with identity and personal brand. What I thought were two polar opposite topics were actually intimately connected.

This book is a culmination of the dualities I have obsessed about with my clients for the last 10 years. Writing it scratched an itch that needed to be scratched and it's been fantastic to articulate these thoughts too. I'm grateful to be helping experts to discover what truly makes them unique and to continue to help them grow and create high-performing businesses from their expertise.

Of course, whilst a book cover has a title and the author's name on the front, it is a big team effort to pull something like this together. There are a lot of people who have helped me and who I owe thanks.

First of all, my family and new husband Mark. You support everything I do, and put up with the endless hours of creating and working to support me in my passion. Thank you for tolerating me and doing all the thankless things that matter.

Mum and Dad, thank you for being everything in this book in action. You are exceptional and have taught me how to be exceptional by having respect, standards and striving to be better every day.

To my team who show up every day and help me to create projects like this book and keep putting myself out there – the only way I can do this is with your support. I am grateful to Monique, MC and Arlene for implementing my crazy ideas and your commitment to helping me support others on their journey.

To the team that have helped pull this book together – Sylvie Blair thank you for putting up with my crazy ideas. Kristen Lowrey for your never-ending patience and sound-boarding support with ideas and editing. This book would not have been ready in time without your advice, work and guidance and working around the clock. I am beyond grateful to have you in my world.

To those who help me with my own identity, hold the mirror up and sparked the idea for this book, being Sally Foley-Lewis and Andrew Griffiths, and to my mentors and mastermind crew, Keith Abraham, Rowdy McLean and Amanda Stevens – I'm so grateful for you all and the journey we are all on together.

To Matt Church, the legacy of your work lives on. Thank you for creating pink sheets so I have a home for all the stuff that goes on in my head! Cha Cha Cha!

Lastly, to my clients past, present and future. Your exceptionality inspires me to keep finding new ways to evolve this work. Thank you for trusting me with your businesses. I'm so grateful to serve and to have found my passion supporting you.

Here's to you discovering your exceptionality. I truly hope that you find it and cultivate it to achieve the impossible!

Jane

Contents

Introduction

'Want a good body? Work at it. Want to be a success? Work at it. Want to be truly exceptional? Be a touch insane... You need a little bit of insanity to do great things.'

– Henry Rollins

I am currently sitting in the airport in Queenstown waiting for a flight back to Brisbane. My husband Mark and I have just spent a week here with my parents and we've had an incredible time. I absolutely love Queenstown. This was my third trip here and I still haven't done everything that I want to. In fact, every time I'm in Queenstown I find more things to add to my list of things to do on the next trip.

Queenstown is my favourite place to visit in the world.

Queenstown is exceptional.

But why? What makes it different?

The beauty of the mountains, the food, the activities, the drives, the creativity.... the food! People travel from all over the world to experience the wonder and joy that is Queenstown.

And what makes it exceptional is that it is wildly unique and world class.

In fact, it's hard to compare it to anywhere else.

But it wasn't always that way.

Mum and dad have vivid memories of what Queenstown was like 45 years ago. And 45 years ago, it didn't look like it does today. It was struggling. And while my parents have memories of it being beautiful, it was seen as a little behind the rest of the western world. It had a tightly held, closed economy. Oil shocks meant skyrocketing prices and the tourism industry was very low. They had one TV channel and the average wage was $95 per week.

In the 1980s, the then prime minister, Labour's David Lange, managed to gain support for a change for New Zealand. He oversaw the transformation of the previously heavily protected New Zealand economy in what was seen as the most radical reform of any economy anywhere in the industrialised world.[1] The Lange government began removing government support of private industry, and privatising previously government-owned commercial activities (such as forestry). They also floated the dollar and the central Reserve Bank was given the responsibility of controlling inflation. This opened up New Zealand to economic growth. Private companies got new opportunities and then created more. New Zealand began to open up.

Close on the heels of this economic reform was the 1988 launch of the world's first commercial bungee jump operation on Kawarau Bridge by Henry van Asch and AJ Hackett.[2] Hackett had already made himself world famous for his guerrilla leap bungee jump off the Eiffel Tower, and the two men were looking for a place where people would embrace

1   Marshall, R and Lange, D. *The Guardian*. 15 August 2005. Accessed at https://www. theguardian.com/news/2005/aug/15/guardianobituaries.obituaries.

2   Davidson, E. 'An Extreme Scene. How Queenstown Became The Adventure Capital Of NZ.' Queenstown New Zealand. Accessed at https://www.queenstownnz.co.nz/ stories/post/an-extreme-scene/.

this kind of experience. They thought Queenstown was the perfect spot. And the opening of bungee jump operation was the start of New Zealand becoming the adventure capital of the world.

These changes were just the start of the newly repositioned New Zealand that you see today. Because of the work that was done to reposition Queenstown on the world stage, today, when you step into Queenstown, you see some of the most exceptional brands in the world. You find extreme adventure and stunning food experiences – incredible fashion and unique retail. From Ferberger's world famous burgers to Patagonia Ice Cream to Antipodes skin care, Botswana Butchery and Armisfield wineries.

New Zealand has found its exceptionality... and because of that, it's powerful positioning. It embraces being wildly unique and world class. And it has become extremely committed to innovation and continuous improvement which has just enhanced that culture of exceptionality.

Notice that the brands that I listed aren't the biggest brands in the world. They don't turn over billions of dollars. Nor are they listed on the stock exchange.

But they are unique *and* have a focus on innovation.

When we are exceptional we hold onto and grow our value. We're not looking to discount and compete on price. We compete on exceptionality. In other words, we outperform our competition by being unique and better than anyone else.

Whether we're conscious of it or not, we all engage with brands, businesses and people who we consider exceptional. We are drawn to people who are exceptional based on what we value. We are drawn to businesses who make great products or who have great services. And we're drawn to people who have great character.

While we're looking for the exceptional, we're also looking for places where we belong. When we're striving towards exceptionality it's to find our own powerful positioning in our own area of expertise.

So we're looking at these brands and people to see if there's something within them that will ignite exceptionality in us. Will that fashion brand elevate my style? Will aligning with that food brand impact my ability to focus on social causes? Will taking a tour with that adventure brand give me a world class life experience?

We all have the ability to be exceptional. And we're all looking for ways to harness that.

But having spent the last 20 years of my career helping people to identify their strengths and in relation to growing their careers and businesses, I can say with confidence that exceptionality is in the everyday.

Let's find that together.

My hope is that this book will inspire you to have the courage to be wildly unique and world class and to ignite your own exceptionality.

Jane

Section 1

The Power of Exceptionality

'Someone who is exceptional in their role is not just a little better than someone else who is pretty good. They are 100 times better.'
— Mark Zuckerberg

Chapter 1

Why Exceptionality Matters?

Years ago, when I was much newer to my practice, I went to hear motivational speaker Keith Abraham speak.

I was so thrilled to be in the same room as him, as he was one of the people that I really looked up to and admired in the consulting space. At that stage, I had never had a paid speaking event and had never spoken in front of more than 50 people. So, I was in awe of him and really felt that I was sitting in the room with genius.

I will never forget the moment in his speech, however, when he began mentioning the many mentors that he had worked with in the past and those he was currently working with now. These people were coaches, advisors and mentors that he used to elevate his own practice.

I was amazed. Keith Abraham is one of the most experienced motivational speakers and experts in Australia but he still seeks out inspiration and support from others. His recognition of his own coaches and mentors was incredibly fascinating to me because he's been doing this work for 30 years, and he's clearly an expert in his field. Yet, he's still talking about learning and growing and trying to continue to be better.

Most people would think, 'Wow, hasn't he already made it?' But from his own perspective he hasn't. He still believes he's a work in progress. He's still learning every day. And he's still working with coaches and consultants, bringing people around him who can help him continue to get better. That is the mindset of an exceptional person.

Over time I've come to realise that the best, most exceptional leaders among us always need mentors. They always need coaches. They always need growth and improvement. And that's because they simply aren't willing to rest on what they already do well.

They're always striving to be better. They're always looking to move from great to exceptional. Because it's this that delivers powerful positioning.

Moving From Great to Exceptional

Keith Abraham is a fantastic example of someone that is always moving along the journey from great to exceptional by continuing to find ways to improve. Likewise when we look at others who have achieved success, such as Ash Barty, Michael Jordan, Jeff Bezos and Jennifer Lopez, we see that despite their success they have never rested on their laurels. Instead, once they've achieved a goal, they're continuously looking for the next thing and obsessed about getting better. This is the essence of exceptionality.

EXCEPTIONALITY MODEL

	ACTIVITY	FOCUS	INFLUENCE	
5	Exceptional	World Class	10x	BEST
4	Evolving	Improvement	5x	BETTER
3	Extraordinary	Uniqueness	2x	DIFFERENT
2	Existing	Safety	1x	BASIC
1	Exiting	Rescue	0x	WORST

ELEVATION

STAGNATION

Anderson

When we look at the above model, we can see that moving from the lower levels up through the higher levels is a function of your activity, and where you're putting your focus. This then affects your level of influence.

Level 1 – Exiting

At this level you feel like you're at your absolute worst – and you're likely performing that way as well. You're avoiding being seen, hoping that no-one will notice the things you feel you lack. You don't have the capacity to think too much and are hoping that perhaps someone will just rescue you from the pain you're in. Your favourite excuse is, 'I think I'm washing my hair that day'. The level of influence you have is non-existent too.

Level 2 – Existing

At this level you're playing safe. You don't want to look incompetent so you avoid rocking the boat and stepping into unchartered waters. You stay with the familiar so you don't take any risks. You want to feel like you belong and are protected from anything that could go wrong. But this also means that your level of influence is very low too.

Level 3 – Extraordinary

Here you are beginning to focus on setting yourself apart from others. You start to consider your strengths, what you do that might be different or better than what others can do. Your self-awareness is growing and you notice the patterns in the roles you have had. You have feelings of ambition and growth and realise you also need to *do* something different if you're to show *how* you are different. The level of influence you have is also beginning to grow along with your focus on becoming better.

Level 4 – Evolving

Once you have identified what makes you unique you decide to hone your craft a little more. You decide to cultivate the skills and look at ways that you can begin to elevate your craft. You decide you want to be better at what makes you different. And you notice that opportunities are opening up for you. As a result you begin to elevate your influence.

Level 5 – Exceptional

The next step is to become exceptional. And to become exceptional you have to focus on being world class. This is about the absolute obsession with stepping into your mastery and becoming the best in the world at what you do. Interestingly, this also means that you never reach your potential. And that's because the best never feel like they have achieved their best (their potential). It's elusive and it's also part of the challenge of making a conscious choice towards continuing wisdom and mastery.

What Does This Mean For You?

When looking at this model, where do you see yourself? What are you focusing on? What level of influence do you feel you have? Implementing the actions that you need to take in order to move up the levels of the exceptionality model is the art of exceptionality.

The Art of Exceptionality

When clients come to work with me, they don't often see their problem as one of 'exceptionality'. They don't usually come to me and say, 'I'm just not as exceptional as I want to be.' Instead, my clients see their biggest challenge as one of positioning. So they often ask questions like:

- How do I cut away from the pack and differentiate myself from everyone else?

- How do I work with the right level in organisations?

- How can I gain more referrals and leads?

- How can I get a high paying job?

- How do I compete? Every time I find my unique positioning, someone comes into the space!

Of course, positioning is part of becoming exceptional. If you want to get there, you need to position yourself as such.

The Problem

We're often told that the best way to position ourselves is through differentiation – demonstrating what makes us unique or special. The problem here is that differentiating yourself simply isn't enough. Pretty soon people catch up to you. And if you're doing something great, they'll begin to copy you.

You might then evolve your business or practice and differentiate yourself again. Only to find the same thing happening... again. So you get tired and frustrated because, despite your hard work, you're simply plain vanilla.

And when you're plain vanilla you aren't getting noticed. You aren't getting the gigs. Or if you are getting gigs, they're just average gigs (while others around you seem to be getting better and better gigs or better and better paying jobs).

The Solution

The world is incredibly noisy today. It's harder to stand out whether you're building a personal brand or a practice, looking to elevate your leadership or simply job seeking. But exceptionality is the key to doing just that.

EXCEPTIONALITY

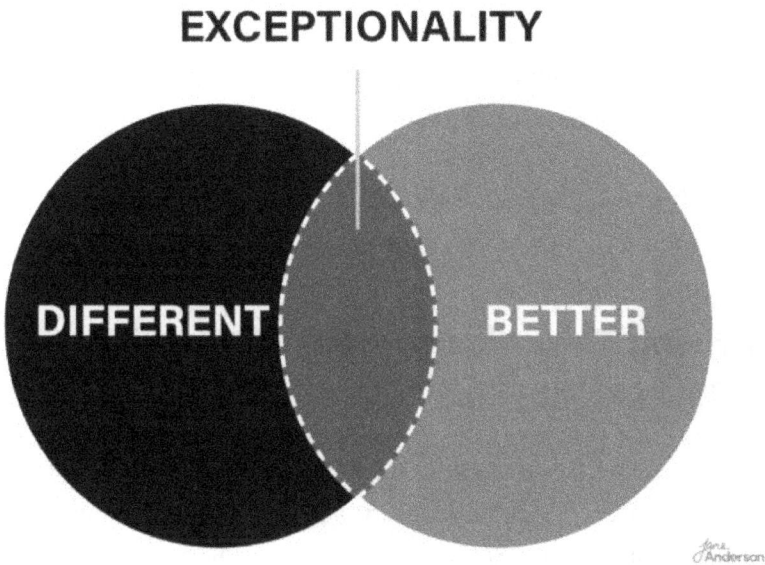

Different + Better = Exceptional

As the model above demonstrates, it's at the intersection of uniqueness (or how you are different) and continuous improvement (or how you are better) that you find your way to exceptionality.

In other words, being different and better makes us exceptional.

The effort we've put into being different or unique hasn't been wasted. This is our first step. And becoming 'wildly unique' as we'll see is a vital part of an exceptional brand and practice. But often people work out how they're unique and then stop there. And that's because they've never been told that being unique is good, but being better is vital.

It's the striving towards improvement – to becoming better – that elevates that uniqueness to the level of exceptionality.

The Dalai Lama said, 'As free human beings we can use our unique intelligence to try to understand ourselves and our world. But if we are prevented from using our creative potential, we are deprived of one of the best characteristics of a human being.'

We all have a unique intelligence and vast creative potential. We just have to tap into it and continue to grow it daily.

Striving Towards Exceptionality – The Progress Principle

How we strive to embrace our creative potential and move towards exceptionality will look different for each of us. Keith Abraham utilised expert mentors and coaches to help him reach his next best self. Maybe courses or upskilling might be the thing for you. Whatever it is, it must be part of your daily activities. You must continuously improve in order to be better.

Research shows that the best way to keep your motivation is to take a step forward every day – even if it's the smallest step you can imagine.[3] In fact, the researchers found that the happiest people – the ones that were the most motivated at the end of the work day – were those that had achieved something... even if it was very small.[4]

This is known as 'the progress principle' and in this book we look at it in terms of 'continuous progression' or 'kaizen'. But at the end of the day it all amounts to the same thing – striving towards exceptionality.

---

3   Amabile, T and Kramer, S. 'The Power of Small Wins.' May 2011. Harvard Business Review. Accessed at https://hbr.org/2011/05/the-power-of-small-wins.

4   Amabile. The Power of Small Wins.

So... Why Does Exceptionality Matter?

Because It Gives You Powerful Positioning.

Why do we bother with all this effort? Why do we bother to push towards exceptionality? Isn't good enough... well, good enough?

Exceptionality matters because being exceptional is what gives you positioning in your area of expertise. Al Ries author of the book, *Positioning: The Battle for Your Mind*, says 'The essence of positioning is sacrifice. You must be willing to give up something in order to establish that unique position.'[5]

Of course Al is referring to the notion that we can't be everything to everybody if we want to have powerful positioning, I'd like to take that further. I'd say you also must be willing to give up on an easy, low-energy practice. You must be ready to do the work required to continuously improve if you want to gain that powerful positioning. In other words, you must be ready to drive towards exceptionality.

You can think of it like pigeons in a pigeonhole. Positioning ensures you're in the right hole (or position) to offer the right services to your clients. And if you're not in the right position, exceptionality helps you climb there.

Years ago I started a new job as Head of Learning & Development in a new company. From my first day there was a particular head of another division that was always rude and abrupt with me. I couldn't figure out why. He didn't know me. I hadn't done any work for him. There seemed to be no explanation.

---

5   Ries, A and Trout, J. (2001). Positioning: The Battle for Your Mind. McGraw Hill.

It turned out that this particular head had disliked working with the person who had held the L&D role before me. He felt that they'd been roadblocks to his ability to get his work done and effect any real change. And when I came into the role – he assumed that I'd be the same. So I had inherited a negative position and found myself in a pigeonhole that I didn't want to be in.

I spent an entire year working hard to prove to him that I was good at my job. More than that – I was exceptional. And because of that, I was able to change the positioning. I was able to change my pigeonhole.

As humans our brains naturally want to organise people into categories. And a confused mind – someone who doesn't understand what you offer, or how you provide it, is far more likely to simply say 'no'. But if you can get your category right through your positioning then you are far more likely to get a 'Yes!'

As Al Ries says, 'Positioning is not what you do to a product. Positioning is what you do to the mind of the prospect.'[6]

Because It Makes Your Referrable

When you are able to get a 'yes' because of your positioning, you're also able to be referred easily. In fact, experts list 'exceeding expectations' as the number one item that makes you referrable.[7] And referral marketing is one of the most important avenues we have of marketing our business.

New research reveals that referral marketing is the most trusted, with 87% of sales marketing efforts resulting in a sale when using B2B referral

---

6   Ries. Positioning.

7   Stec, C. '14 Effective Ways to Get High-Quality Referrals from Your Customers.' 2 August 2021. Hubspot. Accessed at https://blog.hubspot.com/service/how-to-get-referrals.

marketing while only 42% are effective without.[8] Even more, referrals have the highest conversion rates. 71% of sales personnel, 75% of sales leaders and 70% of marketing personnel believe that the majority of B2B companies record a bigger conversion rate from referrals as compared to other channels. Plus, and importantly, referrals end up creating 65% of new business opportunities.[9]

So, being easily referrable is a fantastic way to market your business and drive your own growth.

What Holds You Back?

If becoming exceptional were easy, we'd all be doing it every day. At the end of the day, most of us want to be exceptional. We want to be world class. But it's not easy. And sometimes we're held back, often by the fear of putting ourselves out there. We're held back by a feeling that we might *not* be exceptional. And that people are going to see through us and realise that.

When we embrace these fear-driven ideas and let them take root in our minds, then we're actually creating our own deprivation. We're giving into the noise.

This is something we'll explore in depth in Chapter 3, but it's important to keep it in the front of our minds as we explore exceptionality generally. Because it's easy to get derailed. And the things that could potentially derail us could come up at any time.

---

8   B2B Referral Statistics. 2022. ThinkImpact. Accessed at https://www.thinkimpact. com/b2b-referral-statistics/#:~:text=83%25%20of%20the%20customers%20 are,65%25%20of%20new%20business%20opportunities.

9   B2B Referral Statistics. ThinkImpact.

We are living in an era where we have unprecedented access to opportunity and growth. If there was ever a time to elevate into your exceptionality, it's now. And when you do, the effects will be incredible!

We Can Achieve Our Potential and Yet So Many of Us Never Do

It's my firm belief that we all have the opportunity to achieve our potential – to have the businesses, careers and lives we've dreamt of. Many of us never do and never will. But we are living in an era where we have unprecedented access to opportunity and growth. If there was ever a time to elevate into your exceptionality, it's now. And when you do, the effects will be incredible!

Let's get started!

Key Questions

1. Where are you on the exceptionality scale?

2. How do you know?

3. Why do you want to be exceptional?

4. What would change if you were exceptional?

5. What negative beliefs or stories do you hold about your exceptionality?

6. How will you know your exceptionality is working?

7. What does your exceptionality look like for you?

8. What platforms might you need to use to become exceptional?

9. When do you want to start?

Chapter 2

The Mindset of Exceptionality

'To create something exceptional your mindset must be focused relentlessly on the finest detail.'

— Georgio Armani

Whether you're a speaker, a thought leader, an executive or a consultant, when it comes to being exceptional, your mindset matters. Being exceptional is about more than just doing great work. It's about more than just being a great thinker, or building a great business. It's also about having the mindset of exceptionality. In fact, it's only when you have a mindset of exceptionality that you can achieve exceptionality in the other parts of your practice.

So, what is the mindset of exceptionality, and how do you develop it? And ultimately, how can this demonstrate your uniqueness and elevate your practice?

Being exceptional is about more than just doing great work. It's about more than just being a great thinker, or building a great business. It's also about having the mindset of exceptionality.

The Mindset of Exceptionality

Mindset is one of the first issues we face when elevating our positioning. We're constantly asking ourselves, 'Am I good enough? Am I smart enough?' And too often the imposter can take hold. It gets into our mindset and gives us answers to the negative.

So, to get into the exceptionality mindset, we have to shift our focus to two key areas. These are:

1. What is it that makes you wildly unique?

2. How focused are you on continuous improvement?

Mindset of Exceptionality Model

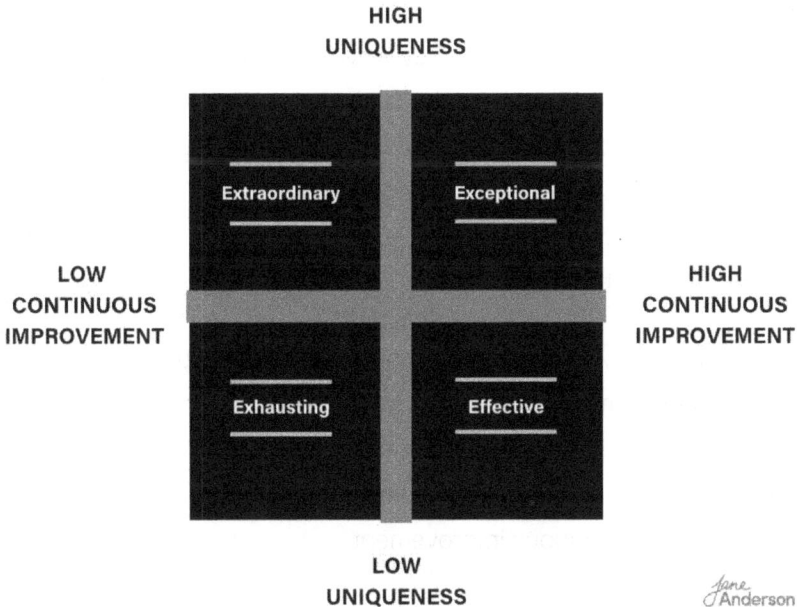

**HIGH
UNIQUENESS**

Extraordinary	Exceptional
Exhausting	Effective

**LOW
CONTINUOUS
IMPROVEMENT**

**HIGH
CONTINUOUS
IMPROVEMENT**

**LOW
UNIQUENESS**

Jane Anderson

Applying the Mindset of Exceptionality Model to the two questions above, we're able to get excellent insight into your current mindset, and what needs to be done in order to improve it.

So, people who have a low differential, or a low level of uniqueness, can be effective if they are also focused on continuous improvement. But if they aren't then they'll just find their work and practice exhausting.

In the same way, if a person has positioned themselves as very unique in their niche but fails to implement a mindset of continuous improvement, then they'll never rise from extraordinary to the highly-desirable level of exceptional.

When I ask my own clients these two questions they are often enough to open them up and help me to see where they fall on the Mindset of Exceptionality Model. For example, their unique point of difference might be resilience because they've overcome incredible hurdles to achieve their expertises. Or perhaps it's their creativity and their ability to have ideas and a vision. Or perhaps it's their ability to gain powerful insights into data and emerging trends. Or perhaps it's the awards they have won in their own niche. Any of these things can be their point of uniqueness and the thing that can ultimately drive their exceptionality.

Once we identify this, we then look to see where they are in terms of continuous improvement. Understanding this helps both of us understand how they are positioned in their own mind. From there, the focus becomes growth, innovation, creativity and how much they obsess about continuous improvement.

The Exceptionality Mental Lens

Your mindset is important as you strive to achieve exceptionality. But your mindset impacts more than that. Your mindset is your mental lens. It dictates what information you take in, it helps you to make sense of the world and it allows you to better navigate the situations that you encounter within your practice.

Your mental lens is totally unique to you and it will impact how you react to any situation. You will likely react differently than another expert and you might feel differently too. And that makes your exceptionality mindset a vital part of developing your positioning and message.

Prioritise Your Mindset Development

If you truly want your practice to become exceptional, you need to prioritise your mindset development. But why?

Research shows that most leadership development programs are not very effective simply because they overlook the vital attribute of mindset.[10] The reverse holds true. When mindset becomes part of your focus, then your ability to be more effective in your life is increased. And that means you'll be in a better position to strive towards an exceptional practice and elevate your influence. Of course, one of the keywords here is *strive*.

Nelson Mandela said, 'Do not judge me by my successes, judge me by how many times I fell down and got back up again.' This is an

---

10   Gottfredson, R and Reina, C. 'Exploring why leaders do what they do: An integrative review of the situation-trait approach and situation-encoding schemas'. February 2020. Leadership Quarterly. Accessed at https://www.sciencedirect.com/science/article/pii/S1048984318308385.

exceptional mindset – one that adopts the progress principle and the idea of continuous improvement.

It's easy when things are going well to just sit back and celebrate your success. But that won't lead you to create more exceptionality in your practice. It's when you experience failures, and you are driven to keep moving forward despite setbacks, that you're able to experience this exceptionality. In fact, when you have an exceptional leadership mindset, you see your failures as a step to eventual success.

Even more, your mindset helps to protect you from negative outside influences. I like to think of it as a padded suit or a bubble suit. When you're in this suit, everything else just kind of bounces off of you.

Your mindset works in this same way. Dan Collins, the former Australian four-time Olympic kayaker, is a great example of mindset. He started with humble beginnings in Blacktown, NSW, but took himself all the way to the Olympic Games four times despite experiencing negative outside influences. He shares now that this was the result of his positive – exceptional – mindset. It was this mindset that allowed him to move past any negative feedback to get to the top of his sport.

How to Use Mindset to Become Exceptional

In order to become exceptional, we need to cultivate and practice an exceptional mindset. We can do this by:

1. Developing a learning mindset

2. Embracing failures and mistakes

3. Building on momentum

Step 1: Developing a learning mindset

Your first step is to develop a learning mindset. This allows you to be open to new processes and new ways of doing things. Importantly, it also helps you adapt to the struggle of continuous improvement because you can see that when you're struggling, you're learning and growing.

You can think about it as learning to write with your non-dominant hand. It will be nearly impossible at first, but as you keep practicing, you will get better and better. It's not necessarily the skill that matters. It's the attitude that learning – even though it's hard – will elevate your capabilities, and when it comes to the mindset, your practice, that really matters.

Step 2: Embracing failure and mistakes

Rather than letting your failures derail you, use them to grow. Use them to show you how to take your practice from where you are now, to where you want to be. And then when you get to the place where you're having lots of success, push forward until you're failing a little bit again. This is how you continue to improve and continue to build exceptionality.

Step 3: Building on your momentum

As your mindset starts to change, and you begin to elevate your practice to become exceptional, keep pushing. Keep growing and developing, and, yes, even struggling. When you have success, it's easy to simply sit back and celebrate your win. But to become truly exceptional, and continue to remain that way, you have to always be pushing forward.

Your Unique Mindset

Ultimately, your mindset is completely unique to you just as your practice is. What you need to do or create within your own thoughts and thought processes is totally dependent on who you are. But it is also your uniqueness that will enable you to grasp that mindset.

In the same way that your uniqueness amplifies your communication, your uniqueness will allow you to embrace, develop and amplify your mindset. Your mindset may even be the unique thing that amplifies that communication as well.

Key Questions

When you're looking to develop your exceptionality mindset, there are some questions to ask yourself:

1. What makes you unique?

2. How much do you obsess about continuous improvement?

3. What mental blocks do you face when wanting to become exceptional?

4. Who do you think is exceptional? How would you describe their mindset?

5. What self-talk do you use to motivate and encourage yourself?

6. Whose story of being exceptional inspires you? What specific areas of their story are exceptional to you?

7. Who has been the most exceptional teacher in your life? What makes them different and better than any other teacher you have had?

8. In what ways did you dream about being exceptional as a child?

9. What beliefs do you hold about people who are exceptional?

Chapter 3

What Holds Us Back From Being Exceptional

'The most common way people give up their power is thinking that they don't have any.'

— Alice Walker

In 2008, I started my life again. My husband at the time was having an affair and rather than being guilt-ridden, he was proud of his actions and would tell anyone who would listen what he was doing. So, I left town, ashamed and embarrassed.

This was also around the time of the global financial crisis and, to add to my upheaval, I couldn't get a job no matter how many I applied for. In fact, applying for jobs started to become a full-time job. At this time, nothing seemed to be going right. I moved home to my parents' house and I remember sitting at my parents' dining table and my mother saying to me, 'I don't know what you're doing but I think it's time you talked to Centrelink.'

Now, I wasn't too embarrassed to do that, but I was already feeling really disempowered. I was feeling like my life was out of control. Things were happening where I didn't feel like I had any choices. And I was finding my circumstances hard to change.

So, I decided to take action. I shifted into my 'put myself out there' approach and began to concentrate on figuring out what kind of company or role resonated as my dream job. I knew there was someone out there who needed my help. I just needed to find them.

I set out on my goal and approached a company that met those criteria. They had a need for the help I could provide, and they were the kind of company I'd always dreamed of working for. They hired me and it was an excellent fit for both of us.

Putting ourselves out there doesn't always come naturally to all of us. And sometimes we may engage in self-sabotaging activities that hold us back from stepping into our personal power. But putting ourselves out there is absolutely vital if we want to become exceptional. We simply cannot strive for more, achieve more or be more, without doing more.

When we can recognise the things that hold us back from putting ourselves out there, from embracing our personal power, then we are in a stronger position to push forward into our exceptionality.

When we can recognise the things that hold us back from putting ourselves out there, from embracing our personal power, then we are in a stronger position to push forward into our exceptionality.

The Four Derailers That Hold Us Back

So what are the 'derailers' or behaviours that often hold people back from stepping into their personal power? There are four primary ones which include:

1. Inadequacy

2. Scarcity

3. Pity

4. Vanity

The Four Derailers Model

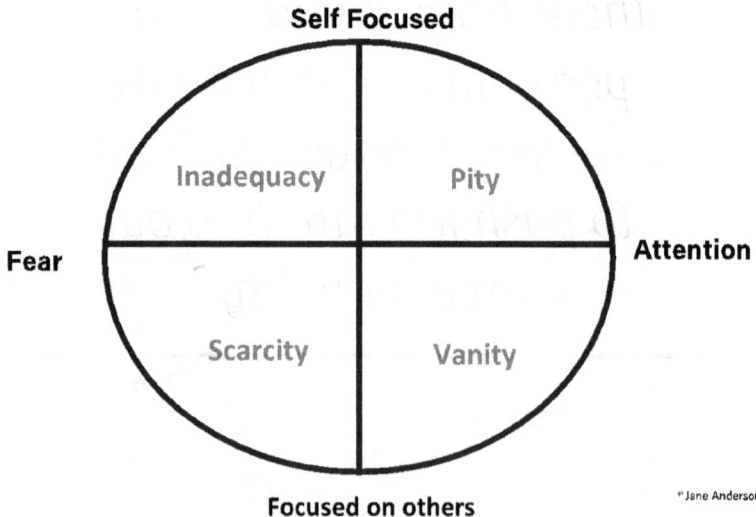

*Jane Anderson

1. Inadequacy

When you are focused on yourself too much, and fearful in your practice then you can suffer from feelings of inadequacy. This is the situation where you feel you're not good enough. Or not smart enough. Maybe you don't have a degree or the experience that some of your competitors do. Or maybe you don't have a huge social media following, or an extensive email list. Whatever the cause, this sense of inadequacy is sometimes called the 'imposter syndrome'.

The imposter syndrome is the name for the fear that someone is going to find you out. That someone is going to look around and realise that you don't belong, and you don't deserve to be there.

If this is you (and it's nearly all of us at some point in our careers), your next step is to answer these key questions:

- Have you started to make steps towards your goals?

- Are the fears you have ones that you have created in your own mind?

- Have you spoken to an expert, mentor or coach with experience to advise you?

- Have you actually had a conversation with a decision maker you're wanting to influence about what you're trying to do and how you can help them?

If you answered no to these questions, then you know what your next step is. To change the no to a yes.

2. Scarcity

Where you are focused on others but still fearful, then you might find yourself feeling scarcity. In other words you feel that there simply isn't enough good work for you.

Scarcity is one of the greatest challenges when trying to step out into your space. When you are looking at the world from a place of scarcity, you'll find yourself distracted by what everyone else is doing. Worse, you might find yourself worrying that all the opportunities have gone, all the jobs are taken, no-one has the money or can afford to hire you.

If this is you, it's time to see if your assumptions are actually true. Are the jobs really all taken? Have the opportunities all gone? More often than not, it simply isn't true. The jobs are there, and the opportunities as well. But perhaps you need some guidance to know the right way to implement your approach. Maybe you need to put your blinkers on and stop comparing yourself to others. Or maybe you just need to pick up the phone and ask the right people the right questions to see if your assumptions are true?

3. Pity

When things don't go the way you want or expect it can be very frustrating. It can seem like no matter what you do, nothing works. You're questioning why this is happening to you or what you've done wrong. And the payoff is that when you share the issue with others, they feel sorry for you, which therefore gains you attention. Sometimes you might start to enjoy the pity, which leads you to seek it out more and more. In this case you are both self-focused and attention seeking – and pity is your reward.

If this is you, it's time to put a deadline on the emotion. It's not going to get you anywhere. Take control by asking for real help if you feel like you can't step out of the situation on your own. Stop being at the peril of your circumstances or playing the victim.

4. Vanity

Sometimes we can become focused on the attention we're getting from others in our practice. Vanity – which is what this essentially is – can become a primary focus in your practice. And that can hold you back.

Yes, seeking validation is natural when gaining a sense of identity, whether personally, in your brand or in your practice. However, when you're struggling under vanity then you might become primarily driven to do things that will bring you that validation. And that means only putting out what's 'popular' (or even neutral). But when you aren't standing in your own uniqueness or embracing your authentic difference, you aren't necessarily being your most powerful you.

How do you know that this is you? Do you constantly seek likes and comments on your social media feed? Do you need to be reassured all the time? Do you look for things that you know your audience will like at the expense of sharing things that align with your brand even if it might challenge others? This is not stepping into your power. This is playing the popularity contest. And when you play the popularity contest you will always remain a follower not a leader.

Avoiding Derailers in Your Practice

Inadequacy, scarcity, pity and vanity – these are heavy derailers to your ability to effectively put yourself out there in order to grow in exceptionality. Instead, you should take active steps to avoid these derailers and step into your own power. Here are some ways you can do that:

Own Your Accomplishments

When you can internalise your successes, then you're better able to protect yourself against imposter syndrome or feelings of inadequacy. When you aren't able to do that, you're at risk for thinking you just got lucky (and worrying that it might not happen again). So be sure to embrace your daily victories.

Keep Driving Forward

It's important to keep the pressure on in your practice. In other words, don't fight feelings of inadequacy or scarcity by lowering the bar. Instead, keep pushing the bar up, keep striving for more and keep continuously improving. If, on the other hand, you do try to take the pressure off by lowering the bar, you'll simply lower your ability to become exceptional.

Embrace Failure

We've talked about embracing failure already, and it will help you to continue to improve. But it will also help you to avoid feelings of inadequacy or even vanity. If you're not afraid to fail, then you won't be afraid to take risks and be your authentic self. When you fail you can rest on the feeling that you're striving, experiencing and growing.

Make Plans

When you fail to plan in your business, you leave yourself open to all the derailers. And that's because winging it just serves to make you feel like a phony. On the other hand, putting in systems, processes and methodologies – as well as setting weekly, monthly, quarterly and yearly goals – will give you a focus and a benchmark.

Often experts don't want to set goals because they're worried that they're just setting themselves up for failure. But if you *don't* set goals, then you will never improve or grow or become exceptional. And, even if you don't meet your goals, even if you do fail, it's simply a stepping stone to becoming better.

Laugh at Yourself

You can't take everything so seriously – even in your practice. If you are totally humourless people just won't resonate with you. And you'll find getting through the day to be quite a slog too.

On the other hand studies show that people like self-deprecating humour by leaders.[11] In fact, leaders who strike the right balance, laughing at themselves but not their colleagues or team, are more likable, trustworthy and caring. And this is a fantastic way to combat the derailers we experience in business as well.

Conclusion

When it comes to embracing a mindset of exceptionality, we always have to be on the lookout for these derailers. They are insidious and sneaky and can rear their heads even when you feel like everything is going well. But if we let feelings of inadequacy, scarcity, pity or vanity creep into our practice, they can easily overwhelm our ability and motivation to seek out the continuous improvement that we need to move onto

---

11   Hoption, C, Barling, J and Turner, N. "'It's not you, it's me": transformational leadership and self-deprecating humor.' 1 February 2013. Leadership & Organization Development Journal. Accessed at https://www.emerald.com/insight/content/doi/10.1108/01437731311289947/full/html.

the next stages of our exceptionality journey – becoming wildly unique and world class.

Key Questions

1. What holds you back from putting yourself out there?

2. What are you most afraid of, really?

3. Which quadrant of the The Four Derailers Model most resonates for you when putting yourself out there?

4. When was a time when you put yourself out there in the past and it went well? What went well? What would you do if you had your time again?

5. When was a time in the past where it didn't go well? What didn't go well? If you had your time again what would you do differently?

Section 2

Wildly Unique

'What makes you different or revered, that is your strength.'
– Meryl Streep

Overview

If you've ever seen an Angostura Bitters bottle with its oversized white label, you'll know it's pretty distinctive. But many people don't know the story behind the bottle's appearance. And it's a story worth telling.

When Dr Johann Siegert died in 1870, his two sons took over the already established bitters business. They wanted to expand the business and gain more widespread attention. So they decided to enter a bitters competition in order to showcase their product's quality to the world.

In preparation for the competition one brother was in charge of designing a new bottle and the other of designing a new label. Unfortunately, they didn't consult each other about sizing and when the new labels and bottles arrived, the label was too big.

Angostura Bitters

It was too late for them to make any changes, so they entered the competition with their bottle covered in the oversized label. They lost the competition, but one of the judges encouraged them to keep their 'signature labelling'.

They did, and since then all Angostura bottles are made and shipped with this recognisable and iconic piece of packaging.

What is Uniqueness?

When it comes down to it, uniqueness has a very simple definition – it's what makes us different from everybody else. And for Angostura that was its label – the result of a series of accidental, yet fortuitous choices.

But there are so many factors that can make us unique in the eye of a customer, sometimes it can be hard to put your finger on the one to focus on. And we're not always as lucky as the Siegert family. So for each of us, the key is to decide which one or ones feel most authentic to you and most relevant to your customer.

To do that you've got to have a really clear intention, purpose and vision about what you're trying to create. Then once you know that, you can identify which of your unique elements are the best ones to help you truly stand out.

Coco Chanel once said that, 'Beauty begins the moment you decide to be yourself.' I think that's so true. Being able to identify who you are and understand what elements play into your unique identity is like identifying your fingerprint. They demonstrate that there's no one else like you on this planet. And that uniqueness is really the value that you bring to your own clients and customers.

When people ask, 'Why wouldn't I work with anybody else? Why wouldn't I buy from anybody else? Why wouldn't I give anybody else the job?' The reason why they wouldn't is because there's no one else quite like you.

I've spent the last 20 years helping people to identify their uniqueness, to better sell themselves and stand out from the crowd. These people have been leaders and doctors, some of the world's best performers and speakers. What I know from having worked with so many different people over these two decades is that the more that we can identify what it is that truly makes them unique, the more we're able to help them get the opportunities and paying gigs. These are the ones who are able to go on and achieve the dreams that they've always dreamt of achieving.

I often think of the scene in *The Greatest Show on Earth*. In it Brad Braden, the no-nonsense general manager of the circus and male lead of the movie, selects the performers for the show. They come from really diverse backgrounds and they have all these quirky and weird things about them. But at the end of the day that's what makes the show so spectacular and so unique – it's the community that is built by these diverse, quirky but, ultimately, extraordinary people. And that's a part of embracing the 'wildly unique'.

There are many people out there who do work around helping people identify their uniqueness. I'm a big fan of Sally Hogshead's work which she sets out in her book, *Fascinate*.[12] In it she talks about being able to identify the elements that play into how the world sees you, as opposed to how we see ourselves.[13] Sally believes that if we can identify how

---

12 Hogshead, S. (2016). FASCINATE: Your 7 Triggers to Persuasion and Captivation. Harper Business.

13 Hogshead. FASCINATE.

the world sees us, then we know how to relate to it. We know how to sell to it. We know how to connect with it. And that means that we can, ultimately, achieve more.[14]

When you're looking for the elements that make you wildly unique, take the following steps:

1. First, ask trusted family, friends or colleagues what they think makes you unique. In other words, what do they think makes you different from everybody else?

2. Second, how do they describe you when you're not in the room? Ask them this question. If you're not there, how do you describe me to other people?

3. Third, what are the things that are coming off the top of their head? This will help you gain a really valuable insight into the thing they associate with you most strongly.

Why Cultivating Strengths for Your Uniqueness Matters

Cultivating your strengths is a vital part of building your practice generally. It makes you more referable, it helps you get more opportunities and gain more influence and it creates pathways for more people to hear what you have to say. It also means that you are finding ways to stand out that are authentic and congruent to you.

When you are in this space you don't feel like you have to keep fixing yourself. Better, people will begin to trust you more.

---

14 Hogshead. FASCINATE.

If you are trying to work on your weaknesses as opposed to your strengths, you're not really cultivating who you are. Instead, you simply end up changing your identity.

However, I often see people focusing on their weaknesses, rather than their strengths. In these cases, they'll end up trying to 'fix' the things they think aren't working for them or where they see gaps in their knowledge or abilities. But this will never work to raise them to the level of exceptional. Because if you are trying to work on your weaknesses as opposed to your strengths, you're not really cultivating who you are. Instead, you simply end up changing your identity.

Research found in Marcus Buckingham's book, *StandOut 2.0*, shares the powerful realisation that to get the most out of yourself and others, you must build on inner strengths.[15] When individuals seek out activities that they get great satisfaction from doing, they tend to be things that they're the most effective at.[16] This is because they are actively using their strengths, which feels more natural and leads to better outcomes and a feeling of accomplishment.[17]

Buckingham says, 'If you want to win, if you want to excel, if you want to stand out, you're going to have to take the few unique things about you that are beautiful and powerful, and take them seriously, and turn them into contributions.'

In my previous career working in a large retail organisation, I had a wonderful woman called Lisa in my team. She had come into the head office from the retail stores. And because of that she had a very unique and valuable perspective where she really understood what it was like

---

15 Buckingham, M. (2015). StandOut 2.0: Assess Your Strengths, Find Your Edge, Win at Work. Harvard Business Review Press.

16 Buckingham, M. '3 proven ways to win at work, says world-renowned talent expert'. 14 January 2019. CNBC. Accessed at https://www.cnbc.com/2019/01/14/marcus-buckingham-3-scientifically-proven-ways-to-win-at-work.html.

17 Buckingham. '3 proven ways'.

to be working on the shop floor. She knew what things worked (and didn't) at the ground level.

Lisa was also heavily tattooed and, being into rockabilly, had quite an individual approach to fashion. She certainly stood out from the crowd, made no apologies for who she was and I really admired her sense of identity and uniqueness.

At the time we had another person join the team – a lady called Mary. When she came to work with us she was quite pompous. Because of Lisa's appearance – her tattoos and fashion sense – Mary believed that Lisa was unprofessional, a poor trainer and had a brash personality.

But Mary had come from a private school upbringing and started her career in banking. Since then, she'd always been in a corporate 'head office' type of environment. This background meant that she didn't really understand the people that were working on the ground level of our retail company. In those environments we had people from all sorts of backgrounds working in a diverse set of areas such as the warehouse, the shop floor and more.

So, when it came to their ability to train our staff, Lisa was far and away the better trainer. Her uniqueness meant that people could relate to her, and she could relate to them. That was reflected in the incredible results that she got from the training. She now leads up the training department here in Australia in part because she's always stayed true to who she is. She's never tried to 'fix' herself or change to meet some idea of what a corporate employee should look like. Instead, she's just maintained her focus on trying to help people become better every day.

She is wildly unique, and that has seen her move from strength to strength and from success to success.

Key Questions

As we get deeper into this wildly unique section my questions to you are:

1. What do you really want to achieve in your life and your career?

2. What is it that you are really striving for and what is the vision for you? (Because if you don't know what that vision is you'll end up focused on fixing the things that are wrong, rather than cultivating the things that are right.)

3. When have you felt like you didn't fit in or belong? What happened? How did you respond?

4. When have you criticised others who don't fit in? What made them different?

5. When have you felt comfortable not trying to fit in?

6. How do you balance uniqueness and belonging in your career and life?

7. Who is someone who you admire for their uniqueness?

8. What beliefs and stories did you learn about uniqueness growing up?

9. How do you manage bias and your own thoughts about others and their uniqueness?

Chapter 5

Wildly Unique Experiences

When it comes to finding your uniqueness there are certain areas that individuals often focus on. These are:

- your relationships

- your experiences

- your culture

- your achievements and awards

- your hobbies

- social object theory

Your Relationships

For some, their relationships and their ability to build and grow relationships, are their point of unique difference. It can seem so obvious and easy to them, but relationship building is an incredible talent. For those who are more technical experts at what they do, relationships just don't seem to come to them innately, and they can struggle to gain insight and understanding about them.

But relationships are very important. And if you are good at building them – particularly if you are uniquely good – it's a little bit like being glue. You have an incredible ability to bring people together and keep them together to help them to flourish, grow and achieve connection.

As Wayne Dyer, American self-help author and a motivational speaker, said, 'Loving people live in a loving world. Hostile people live in a hostile world. Same world.' When you can bring like people together into a community that embraces them, it's an incredibly wonderful and utterly unique skill that plays directly into your exceptionality.

Exceptional Relationship Building

An exceptional example of relationship building is Dr Justin Coulson. He is a parenting expert, and as a parenting expert he's found global fame. But there are many parenting experts. What sets Dr Coulson apart, what makes him truly unique, is his focus on family relationship building.

Another example is Alena Bennett. She has an accounting background and once worked with some of the biggest consulting firms in the world, including in Australia, the US and overseas. During her career she noticed that what set her apart from others was her ability to understand people. She had a skill at building relationships between herself and others and among others she brought into her circle as well. When she left accountancy, she brought this unique skill with her.

Today she helps people, particularly CFOs, to build careers of the future through relationship building. And it's this understanding of people and how those relationships work that sets her apart.

Relationships – both in and out of the workplace – help to ensure that we enjoy our jobs, spend more time working in them, have better performance outcomes, have an increased perception of social impact and even experience lower job stress.

Thought Leadership, Relationships and Exceptionality

Research shows that strong relationships are a vital part of the quality and success of collaborations.[18] So, when we're looking to collaborate with others, or communicate our thought leadership or expertise to our clients and audience, having strong relationships is a vital part of the process, easing the way. In fact, relationships – both in and out of the workplace – help to ensure that we enjoy our jobs, spend more time working in them, have better performance outcomes, have an increased perception of social impact and even experience lower job stress.[19]

Having this as part of your stable of skills is an excellent way to elevate your performance from good to exceptional. Not only do you have more people in your life to learn from and to collaborate with, but your ability to bring others together expands your reputation for doing just that and this has the effect of raising your profile as well.

Relationship Questions

1. When it comes to relationships are you consulted for your ideas and thoughts?

2. What are you generally consulted about?

3. What do you wish people could see about relationships? Why aren't their relationships working? What could they be doing better?

---

18 Bilmes, J. 'Chaos in kindergarten.' October 2012. Educational Leadership. Accessed at https://eric.ed.gov/?id=EJ1002450.

19 Tran K, Nguyen P, Dang T and Ton, T. 'The Impacts of the High-Quality Workplace Relationships on Job Performance: A Perspective on Staff Nurses in Vietnam.' 23 November 2018. Behavioural Sciences. Accessed at https://www.ncbi.nlm.nih.gov/pmc/articles/PMC6316783/.

4. How do you cultivate your relationships at work and outside work?

5. Who do you spend most of your time with?

6. Who inspires and lights you up the most in your network?

7. When do you draw on your networks and relationships the most?

8. Where are your networks? Where do those in your network live and work?

9. What skills do your networks and the people you hang out with have?

These questions can often be an indicator that relationships might be an area of unique expertise for you to set yourself apart.

Your Culture

To you it may not feel like anything special, but the places that you've lived in the world – and the cultures that have become a part (even a small part) of who you are – can be a fantastic way to demonstrate how you are wildly unique.

There are two reasons for this. The first is that as you travel and live abroad you learn about the world and embrace new experiences. These experiences ultimately help you to engage better with others and understand different viewpoints. But the second is where it gets interesting. Research shows that international experiences actually transform your sense of self.

Learn About the World

Let's talk about the first prong. Living in other cultures, and moving around the world, is a unique experience to you. No one will have had the same combination of experiences that you do.

These experiences help you to uncover your strengths, such as your ability to build relationships, experience inclusion and loneliness, breach language barriers, rely on your resilience and face other challenges to your beliefs, values and resourcefulness. They also give you a path for reaching out and communicating with others as you gain incredible stories around your experiences and learnings by being confronted with things you've never done before and people you've never met, seen or spoken to before.

Ralph Waldo Emerson said, 'Culture opens the sense of beauty.' And I don't think he means physical beauty. I believe he's referring to that opening of our understanding of the nuances of other cultures that lead us to see the beauty there – regardless of where or what it is. And being able to see this makes you unique.

Jessica Schubert is a wonderful part of my community. She is an expert in leadership and specifically works with global multinationals to help them to build their leadership capability in their organisations so they can be better prepared for the future of work. Jessica is a great example of the benefits of international exposure because she has lived in five countries – Japan, Australia, Germany, Hong Kong and Singapore. And those experiences have created a unique perspective which allows her to perform exceptionally well within global multinational organisations.

Part of that success is certainly because she's often been to and worked with people from the countries before. This means that she understands diverse cultural impacts and how to best communicate and connect. She also knows how to adapt her programs and change up the way that she thinks through problems and solutions.

Her unique perspective makes her more saleable and 'easy to buy'. In the first place, people understand how to 'buy' a leadership expert. It's a category that people are already familiar with. But leadership experts are a dime a dozen. And what sets Jessica apart, and makes her wildly unique, is her global expertise. After all, she's not only delivered programs in those countries, she's actually lived in them.

International Experiences Transform Your Sense of Self

The other way that international experiences contribute to you becoming wildly unique, is their ability to transform your sense of self. Studies have shown that 'international experiences can enhance creativity, reduce intergroup bias and promote career success',[20] all things that Jessica's lived experience demonstrates for us. But it also leads to greater 'self-concept clarity'.[21]

What does this mean? Well, in essence, people with greater self-concept clarity understand themselves better. They know their own values and beliefs and can see them as separate from the culture around them.

How does this happen? When people live in their home country, they live their lives surrounded by others who mostly behave in similar ways

---

20 Adam, H, Obodaru, O, Lu, J, Maddux, W. and Galinsky, A. 'How Living Abroad Helps You Develop a Clearer Sense of Self'. 22 May 2018. Harvard Business Review. Accessed at https://hbr.org/2018/05/how-living-abroad-helps-you-develop-a-clearer-sense-of-self?hsCtaTracking=7848c3f4-a1dd-4c18-9be5-a3b929278b1b%7C69a13747-47f7-427a-b82d-8de60af5d3d6.

21 Adam. 'How Living Abroad Helps You Develop a Clearer Sense of Self'.

and have similar beliefs and values. People in their home environment are not forced to question their own core values or behaviours because they are just the way the world is. On the other hand, research found that when people live in other cultures, they become exposed to 'novel cultural values and norms' which prompts them 'to repeatedly engage with their own values and beliefs' and either strengthens them or pushes them to discard them.

Gaining clarity around your own values, beliefs and desired behaviours separate from your culture allows you to inhabit a place where no one else is because they are uniquely you. In fact, they are wildly, uniquely you. You can think of it like a third-dimension to your personality – one that allows you to see things in a brand new way. And once you can do that, you can build your brand around it and share it with the world.

Culture Questions

1. Where have you traveled or lived?

2. What experiences have you had?

3. What is your favourite place in the world to visit?

4. What place is on your bucket list?

5. What languages do you speak?

6. What has been your most memorable travel experience?

7. Who do you like to travel with?

8. What type of travel do you enjoy? Summer, beachy type travel? Winter wonderland? Or adventure?

9. How does this set you apart from everyone else?

Your Achievements and Awards

Sometimes we meet people who have done incredible (exceptional!) things. They may be business people, Olympians, celebrities or even those who have achieved amazing feats, such as climbed Mount Everest, won Australian of the Year or been awarded presidential medals and awards. If this is you, these awards and achievements create social proof. They are endorsements that demonstrate to others that you are unique.

In other words, achievements are like a stamp of approval. They give approval from a trusted third party that says that this person does something better and uniquely different than everybody else. It says that this person is truly exceptional. And they are extremely valuable in setting you apart and defining your unique value in a noisy world.

Maya Angelou said, 'All great achievements require time'. And these achievements are so valuable because not everybody invests the time that you have in order to reach your achievement.

Sharing Your Unique Achievements

Sharing your unique achievements allows you to demonstrate your uniqueness and, more, demonstrate your exceptionality. For example, Sally Hogshead's book, *Fascinate*, which we discussed earlier in this section, is a *New York Times* bestseller and has won over 100 marketing awards. Those awards show everyone that this is an exceptional book worthy of their time.

Rowdy McLean built a business, sold the business and retired all by the age of 34. He then went on to win numerous awards in his space of motivational change. Again, this is external social proof of his expertise.

Ronnie Benbow is the founder and CEO of The Carers Foundation, a not-for-profit charity based in Australia, which is designed to support carers who are caring for disabled or unwell family. And she has won countless awards in this space. In fact, she was nominated for Queenslander Australian of the Year and won Citizen of the Year. As with Sally and Rowdy, these awards demonstrate to others that she is the authority in this space.

For each of these individuals their work is an inspiration. But it's their awards that really set them apart from everyone else in their space. These achievements are the things that let others recognise their exceptionality.

Awards and Achievements Questions

1. What awards have you won?

2. If you were to win any award you could, what would it be?

3. If you were to give out awards what would be the name of the award?

4. What categories of awards are best for what you want to be known for?

5. How can you bring them to the fore so that people are aware of them more?

6. What awards do you perhaps need to win to elevate your uniqueness?

7. If you had a trophy cabinet of awards what would be in the cabinet?

8. If you were to give yourself an award what would it be for?

9. What achievement are you most proud of?

Hobbies

Al Yankovic once said, 'My hobbies just sort of gradually become my vocation.' And while this sounds a little casual, your hobbies are actually another great pathway to discover your individual strengths and uniqueness. This is because they provide a creative outlet that signals to your audience your inner values.

Hobbies are also a valuable connector. They allow your audience to relate to you and to find common ground that you might not have otherwise found.

Marcus Buckingham has done a great deal of research on the power of hobbies in his book, *Love and Work: How to Find What You Love, Love What You Do, and Do It for the Rest of Your Life.*[22] He refers to these hobbies as 'things you love' and describes them as the red threads that tie together everything that you do.

These red threads are the things that come easily to you and give you energy. And when you work these into your life and your work you will find that you are triggered into 'flow' and will become fully immersed in the thing that you're doing. You will no longer feel drained, but find yourself motivated and passionate about what you do.

---

22 Buckingham, M. (2022). Love and Work: How to Find What You Love, Love What You Do, and Do It for the Rest of Your Life. Harvard Business Review Press.

One fantastic example is Anton van der Walt. Anton van der Walt is a leadership expert originally from South Africa. He was previously the HR Manager for Ford in the Middle East and now lives in Australia.

As part of his practice, Anton wrote a fantastic book called *Leadership Through My Lens*[23]. In this book he leverages his hobby – which is a passion for photography, in particular, South African animals. He uses the animals he photographs, and their traits and behaviors, as leadership metaphors in his book. His book is spectacular and it really embraces his passion and enthusiasm for his hobby which lets him stand out in his work as well.

Renee Giarrusso, who is also an expert in leadership, is another great example. She loves to cook and is very creative with her cooking. She leverages her hobby by sharing interesting and evocative metaphors about cooking in her leadership programs. Again, this helps her to be memorable and unique.

Hobbies help you to develop your unique positioning and build a robust brand because they help you connect with people at a human level. And people want that. They want to discover interests in common with you.

We have an English bulldog, and I personally have a passion for bulldogs generally. I've always really loved them and now that I've finally got my own beautiful Winston, I have become very involved in the British bulldog community. I'm active in Facebook groups and organise and attend meetups and other things like that. This is one of my great 'hobbies' and I often bring in some metaphors of that in my own work.

What I have found is that a lot of clients that come to work with me also have dogs, and they love working with another dog owner. It creates a

---

23   van der Walt, A. (2017). Leadership Through My Lens: Volume 1. Bookbaby.

deeper sense of connection when I'm working with them. I make note of their dogs' names, their birthdays, as well as the clients' birthdays. Our entire team really sees dogs as very special creatures and it connects me to them at a different level.

Mark Zuckerberg has been known to ask interviewees about their hobbies and side projects. He says it's the best way to show passion and leadership. And, at the end of the day, hobbies are like a connector to the heart of your audience. They humanise you and your brand and make you really authentic and real.

Hobbies Questions

1. What do you like doing most outside of work?

2. Do you engage in your hobbies alone or with others? If you do spend hobby time with others, who?

3. What specifically do you enjoy most about the hobbies you have? Is it the creativity? Or the action?

4. How often do you get to spend time on your hobby?

5. Where are there communities and groups of people who also enjoy your hobby?

6. How long does your hobby take to do? A day, a week, a year?

7. Are there certain goals to achieve in your hobby?

8. Is it a new or old hobby for you? How long have you been interested in your hobby?

9. Now that you know what you like, how can you elevate it into your branding and positioning to help you to

stand out, be unique and become more connected to your audience?

Social Object Theory

Now we have covered the elements you can use to move from unique and different and from extraordinary to exceptional. But how do you engage with others to see those elements within you? We can tackle that by understanding Social Object Theory.

What is Social Object Theory?

We often think of connection as human to human. But Social Object Theory (SOT) claims that connection is actually based on a separate social object or 'thing'.

Researchers define SOT as 'the belief that all successful social media interactions and ventures center on an object'.[24] They posit that the reason people connect with each other and not someone else comes down to a single social object that is the centrepiece of what they have to talk about. These objects create meaning, purpose and connection, and are often linked to shared beliefs, values and attitudes which are discovered as people connect.[25]

---

24 McDonald, I. Social Object Theory: The Secret Ingredient for Powering Social Influence Marketing Campaigns. 2009. University of Alaska Anchorage. Accessed at http://www.cbpp.uaa.alaska.edu/afef/social_object_theory. htm#:~:text=Engestr%C3%B6m%20described%20social%20object%20 theory,between%20two%20or%20more%20people.

25 McDonald. Social Object Theory.

For example, I go to our local dog park with our English bulldog, Winston. And there's a gentleman there called Lucky Lux who is an artist. If I walked past Lux in the street, I wouldn't even know who he was. But I do because his dog is called Marble and our dog is called Winston and they're friends at the park. So the social object between us is dogs and we've connected over it. Otherwise Lux and I would never have met.

It's the same notion when you follow somebody on social media. You follow them because of their thinking and their ideas, not just because of who they are. And the content that they put out is typically around the social object.

I like to think of social object theory as being like a table that allows us to sit together and have a conversation. It brings people together for a shared purpose – whatever that purpose might be – and lets us have a conversation that we might not otherwise have.

Identifying Your Uniqueness with SOT

When you are working to develop your uniqueness, a big part of that is identifying the social objects around you that help you create a connection between yourself and your audiences. The researcher behind this work, Graham Moore said, 'Art is a social object, books and films and records and television are social objects. There are things that bring two people together in a conversation. I love the notion that I could write something that two people could share, that's the goal.'

Social Object Theory Questions

1. What elements of your brand are social objects?

2. Which of these do you value the most?

3. What do you need to do to develop your social objects?

Conclusion

No matter what area your unique brand element derives from – whether it's your relationships, experiences, culture, achievements and awards, hobbies or social objects – finding that thing will help you to build connections and trust. And those connections will do more for you than any other element of marketing now or in the future. And it will allow you to grow your practice exponentially and go from good to exceptional.

Chapter 6

Wildly Unique Mindset

As we've discussed, we're often told that the best way to position ourselves is through differentiation – demonstrating what makes us unique or special. But of course, differentiating yourself simply isn't enough. The only way to truly rise above the competition, to truly be exceptional, is to be wildly unique.

Becoming Wildly Unique Begins With Mindset

This phrase – 'wildly unique' – really fills me with joy. The word 'wild' can mean so many things, but the one that really resonates with me here is an uninhabited or uncultivated place. And that's exactly where you need to go in order to be exceptional – to the 'uncultivated' place, where no one else is, and where no one else has made their mark.

Of course, as we've discussed, people will catch up to you. Especially when you're doing something new and great. They'll be watching you, following you and nipping at your heels. But that's OK because when you're wildly unique you're already on the way to being exceptional. And when you're exceptional, no one can touch you.

The word 'wild' can mean so many things, but the one that really resonates with me here is an uninhabited or uncultivated place. And that's exactly where you need to go in order to be exceptional – to the 'uncultivated' place, where no one else is, and where no one else has made their mark.

But how do you become wildly unique? What are the steps you should take, or the elements you need to cultivate? In other words, how do you go from unique and different – to extraordinary and exceptional?

First, it begins with mindset.

Why Mindset Matters

Just as we discussed in Section 1, if you truly want your practice to become exceptional, you need to prioritise your mindset development first and foremost.

I often find that mindset is one of the first issues I face when I'm working with thought leaders, speakers, experts and consultants. So I often need to get into their unique leadership mindset. To do that, I'll ask two questions:

1. What frustrates you most about people who don't achieve their goals?
2. What do you wish you had done differently along your own journey?

These two questions are often enough to open them up and give me insight into their mindset and how to develop it. For example, their frustration might be that people aren't very compassionate. Or that they don't work hard enough. Or that they don't live in the moment.

Understanding these frustrations helps me to understand their perspective. And once you find out where their mindset is, you can determine how to turn it into a leadership mindset of exceptionality.

How to Develop an Exceptional Mindset

Mindset really lies in two parallel paths.

1. First, building your brand around your unique mindset can elevate it from vanilla to world-class.

2. Second, having an 'exceptional' mindset allows you to become a world-class brand.

Building Your Brand Around Your Unique Mindset

Take the example of Janine Shepherd. In 1996 Janine was on track to join the Olympics as a cross-country skier. But one day while she was training in the Blue Mountains she was hit by a truck which caused devastating injuries. She suffered a broken neck and her back was broken in six places. She also broke five ribs, her right arm, her collarbone and some bones in her feet. Plus, she had extensive external and internal trauma and massive blood loss.

Janine was told that the only reason she survived was because she was in such peak physical condition. She says, 'I think maybe all the training I'd done up to that point was to prepare me for surviving this accident.'[26]

But she couldn't walk. Even after spending six months in the spinal ward, and recovering in many ways, she hadn't been able to relearn how to walk. One day, as she was sitting in her wheelchair, unable to walk, her Olympic dreams shattered, she heard a plane fly overhead. She decided then that just because she couldn't walk didn't mean that she couldn't fly.

---

26 Shepherd, J. 'Athlete Janine Shepherd's devastating injury and slow road to recovery.' Conversations with Richard Fidler. 23 March 2007. ABC. Accessed at https://www.abc.net.au/local/stories/2007/03/23/1879844.htm.

So, she learned how to do just that and become a pilot. And not just any pilot – but an aerobatics pilot. Eventually she even became the youngest and first female director of the Civil Aviation Safety Authority. And she did learn to walk again, despite being told that she never would.

Janine demonstrates one of the strongest mindsets I have ever witnessed. To become an Olympic level athlete shows incredible mindset. But when that was taken from her, she was then able to envision a new path for herself – one that demonstrated that she didn't just have a strong mindset, but an exceptional one.

Since then Janine has built a brand around mindset, particularly in light of what she's been able to achieve. She's worked tirelessly to raise awareness of spinal cord injury and research. She's presented her message of human potential and resilience to organisations across the globe. And she's a best-selling author. Her work has also seen her awarded Australia's highest civilian acclaim – the Order of Australia.

Her message inspired, and continues to inspire, her audiences to overcome adversity and take on life's challenges. She demonstrates how having an exceptional mindset can propel you into territory that no one else can ever even hope to inhabit.

Having an Exceptional Mindset Allows You to Become a World-Class Brand

To become a world-class brand, you have to have a mindset that will get you there. In fact, experts believe that the 'single most important factor influencing a person's success – whether personal or professional – is mindset'.[27]

---

27 Mariama-Arthur, K. 'Why Mindset Mastery is Vital to Your Success.' 24 February 2017. Entrepreneur. Accessed at https://www.entrepreneur.com/article/285466.

People who struggle with challenges often believe that they are the way they are and simply can't change. Researchers describe this as having a fixed mindset.[28] This is a dangerous place to be because it prevents you from developing and growing in the face of challenges. For example, if Janine had a fixed mindset – if she'd believed that she was 'only good at skiing' – then losing the ability to compete in that sport would have completely sabotaged her health and happiness.

On the other hand, people with a growth mindset – or what we'd call an 'exceptional mindset' – are willing to try new things even if they're hard at first, or if they fail the first time they try.[29] To them this is just a challenge to overcome, rather than something that they'll never be good at. And failure gives them the incentive to continue to develop their skills.

Again – it helps to think of mindset as a padded suit. It's what sits around you helping you absorb the impacts from the world around you. When you have a growth mindset your padded suit is set to reflect the negative beliefs around challenges (i.e., 'why bother, I'm just going to fail' type thoughts). With your padded suit, you still face challenges, but the negativity bounces off, and instead of wallowing, you just look for the next step in your own journey. Instead of thinking, 'why bother', you begin to think, 'how can I improve?' 'How can I become better?'

That is an exceptional mindset.

---

28 Dweck, C. 'The Choice to Make a Difference.' 18 January 2019. Perspectives on Psychological Science. Accessed at https://journals.sagepub.com/doi/10.1177/1745691618804180.

29 Dweck. 'The Choice to Make a Difference.'

Practicing the Exceptional Mindset

Of course, in order to become exceptional, we need to cultivate and practice an exceptional mindset. We set this out in Section 1 and the process remains the same. Develop a learning mindset so you are open to new processes and new ways of doing things. Then accept and learn from your failures, rather than letting them derail you. And finally keep pushing. Keep building on your momentum to elevate your practice to the exceptional.

In this way you will build your unique leadership mindset and amplify your positioning, your messaging and your communications with your community.

Mindset Questions

1. What frustrates you most about people?

2. What do you wish they'd do differently?

3. How can you raise your leadership mindset to build exceptionality within your practice?

Your Perspective and Worldview

I want to move onto perspective and worldview because it's so closely connected with culture. We all have a worldview. And our worldview is formed from the experiences we have and the beliefs we cultivate as we go through our lives.

I often think of worldview as a pair of glasses that are customised to each of us. Our unique set of glasses might have blue lenses, or pink, or be shaded or clear. And how they are made impacts how we see the world.

In this case, however, our 'lenses' are in fact our individual 'collection[s] of attitudes, values, stories and expectations about the world around us, which inform our every thought and action'.[30] You can think of worldview as how our culture plays out in our individual lives. In other words, we go through our experiences and earn our beliefs, and these shape how we see the world and, more importantly, interact in the world.

Researchers say that our worldview is active when we come upon a situation and think, 'That's just wrong'.[31] And that's because we have a natural tendency to think that what we believe is normal or widely accepted by others. On the other hand, anything that goes against what we believe, we tend to see as backwards, uninformed or simply untrue.

Obtaining an Elevated Worldview

For each of us our unique worldview allows us to see and interpret the world. But for some, perhaps those who have come from experiences, or cultures or belief systems that are highly differentiated, that worldview is even more elevated. This elevated worldview lets those unique individuals interpret the world in new and innovative ways. And as Henry David Thoreau said, 'It's not what you look at that matters, it's what you see.'

---

30 Gray, A. 'Worldviews.' 1 August 2011. International Psychiatry. Accessed at https://www.ncbi.nlm.nih.gov/pmc/articles/PMC6735033/.

31 Gray. Worldviews.

A great example of someone with this highly unique worldview is futurist Gihan Perera. In his work as a futurist he focuses on innovation and elevating standards for people and for organisations. He has meticulous attention to detail, is prolific in creating his content and, as a result, he perpetuates his worldview – which is one of elevating standards – with elevated standards himself.

Worldview Questions

Draw a timeline of events in your life:

1. Which ones are the most significant to you, regardless of whether they are good or bad?

2. What theme ties them together?

3. What do you notice that could be an insight into your worldview?

Character

Resilience and how you cope or have dealt with a challenge or situation in your life can be a great inspiration for others and something that can really set you apart.

From an authenticity perspective it's all very well to be able to put content out and say all these things about yourself. But it's when your brand is put under pressure, and tests your ability to cope under that pressure, that perspective becomes the key defining characterisation of who you are and what makes your brand wildly unique. This is the true test of your authenticity and drives the congruence with your branding and messaging.

Helen Keller said, 'Character cannot be developed in ease and quiet. Only through experience of trial and suffering can the soul be strengthened, ambition inspired and success achieved.'

Jelena Dokic is a great example of a brand defined by character. She is a tennis player who performed under incredible pressure from her father. But it went well beyond pressure to win. She actually suffered physical and mentally abuse at his hands as well.[32] At one point he even beat her unconscious.[33]

The abuse that she had to deal with from him still impacts her today. But her resilience and ability to keep going, despite the circumstances, is a defining element of her brand. She's very vulnerable and she shares her message widely, speaking out about her mental health challenges. Her openness about her personal struggles, her ability to share her story and the way she uses her strong character to move forward, creates incredible empathy and helps people to feel aligned to her story. She's shown such an incredible ability to pick herself up and keep moving, and the world embraces her for that strength.

Another example is Joanne Love in our community. Joanne Love is a high-performance expert and an Olympic and Paralympic coach. She specialises in working with swimmers to generate high performance and works extensively with the Australian swim team. She is also part of the executive team for Swimming Australia.

---

32 'Jelena Dokic details father Damir's abuse in new autobiography, alleges she was beaten unconscious'. 12 November 2017. ABC. Accessed at https://www.abc.net.au/news/2017-11-12/jelena-dokic-details-abuse-at-hands-of-father-damir/9142112.

33 'Jelena Dokic'. ABC.

Joanne often talks about the level of resilience that paralympians have. She talks about specific goals and how they set their goals, particularly around goals that they can control. Her research has shown that goal setting actually improves the athletes own mental health and wellbeing.[34]

Research also shows that 'associating your product with a strong brand identity is a key factor in competitive advantage and leads to great financial rewards.'[35] And, like Helen Keller, Jelena Dokic and Joanne Love show us how the strong character traits identified with their brand have driven them from success to success. They are memorable, identifiable and wildly unique... for all the right reasons.

Character-defined branding often makes me think about when I worked for the Sir Robert Mathers family in their retail shop. Occasionally we had somebody who would come in with a faulty pair of shoes who might ask for a refund or replacement. Some of the staff, I used to find, would get their backs up, get a little bit defensive or even become argumentative with a customer. But I always thought that these 'mistakes' were an opportunity to turn the experience around and really define the brand in the best way.

Defining Your Brand When Things Go Wrong

Defining your brand when things go wrong is one of the best ways to establish your unique character.

What do you do when things go wrong? How do you respond to things? Do you respond well? Are you stressed? Are you frustrated? Do you

---

34 Love, J. (2019). Win from Within: Coaches Guide. Proactive Performance Australia.

35 Mindrut, S, Manolica, A and Teodora Roman, C. (2015). 'Building Brands Identity'. Procedia Economics and Finance. Accessed at https://www.sciencedirect.com/science/article/pii/S221256711500088X.

lose your temper? Or do you listen to the customer? How can you use this moment? This moment defines your brand. Are you managing it in the best way? Do you really want to try and see if you can resolve this for the customer?

I think returns, if you're in a retail type business, is one of the key moments that really defines the character of the brand. When you see how brand owners and managers talk about returns in forums, particularly on Facebook and other social media platforms, they're primarily complaining. And they make it quite hard for their customers to seek a return.

But I believe that the easier you make those things, the more you build on the character of a brand. You don't want people taking advantage, obviously, but you've got to be a little bit reasonable. If you can do that, I think customers become more loyal to you because they see that you are actually acting in their best interests.

This idea carries across to service providers as well. As a leadership coach you might have someone who is unable to continue with the full round of coaching that they agreed to. Could you find a way to return some of the money to them, or provide them with something of alternative value. Being helpful and reasonable, and trying to find the best solution for your client, will go a long way to ensuring their loyalty and commitment to your brand.

Character Questions

1. What adversity have you faced that people find inspiring?

2. How did you get through those times?

3. What mindset did you have?

4. What strategies did you use?

Remember that no matter how much you might think that everybody does these character-defining things, most people don't. So the more you can define it, the better your strength of character will be and the more you will stand out authentically.

Chapter 7

Wildly Unique Presence

There are many definitions of presence, including 'the impressive manner or appearance of a person'.[36] So, presence can be thought of as something that inspires confidence and trust in others – and someone who has presence as a person that inspires confidence and trust in others. And when it comes to demonstrating your uniqueness within your brand, it can be a powerful and unique skill.

Whether you're a leader or a communicator, your presence – or your ability to project confidence and authority – sets you apart from the competition. Presence is akin to a lighthouse. It shines the light that guides others when they might otherwise stumble around in the dark. And this shining light gives the person an immense influence on others, as you guide them where you shine your light.

As Gabrielle Bernstein says, 'Your presence is your power.' So, when you can balance warmth and confidence – shining bright like a lighthouse – you create a unique value proposition that demonstrates what it is that you do differently to your audience and community.

---

36 'Presence.' Oxford English Dictionary, Oxford University Press, 2022. Accessed at https://www.google.com/search?q=practice&rlz=1C5CHFA_enAU864AU864&o-q=practice&aqs=chrome..69i57j0i433i512j46i131i175i199i433i512j0i433i512l3j69i-61j69i60.1097j0j9&sourceid=chrome&ie=UTF-8.

Presence is akin to a lighthouse. It shines the light that guides others when they might otherwise stumble around in the dark. And this shining light gives the person an immense influence on others, as you guide them where you shine your light.

A fantastic example of a brand with light-shining presence is Louise Mahler. Louise is a keynote speaker and an expert in executive presence and communication. Her own presence stems from her time as an opera singer. She still sings, of course, but today she uses her skills learned on the stage to teach others how to use their voices and their innate presence to create influence and authority.

Louise is hugely sought after in this role as presence is something that is sometimes hard to nail down. She works with prime ministers, politicians and c-suite executives. She's a secret weapon that not many people talk about but many, many rely on.

In Sylvia Ann Hewlett's book, *Executive Presence*, she says, 'Executive presence is the missing link between merit and success.'[37] Research shows that many leaders focus too much on 'hard' skills, such as operational effectiveness or budget management.[38] But in order to truly succeed they also need to focus on 'soft' skills, such as their ability to influence others through their presence.[39]

Presence Questions

1. Do you find yourself asked to present or deliver key messages on behalf of others?

2. What do you do to project power, authority and influence in your role?

---

37 Hewlett, S. (2014). Executive Presence: The Missing Link Between Merit and Success. HarperCollins.

38 Sherman, R. (2015). The importance of executive presence. American Nurse Today. Accessed at https://www.researchgate.net/publication/277132277_The_importance_of_executive_presence.

39 Sherman. The importance of executive presence.

> 3. What can you do differently?

In the rest of this chapter we'll dive into the elements that you can use to develop presence in yourself and your brand. And this presence could be the X factor that begins to set you apart from your competitors and establish your wild uniqueness.

Your Body

Your body – as an element of presence – is one of those possible X factors. I don't mean how you look, but what you can do and have done with your physical body. Some people just have a real gift to be able to do physical things that are unimaginable for most of us. Perhaps you do too – whether it's your sailing prowess, how far you can run or the mountains you've climbed. This can set you apart because people find it fascinating and inspiring to see the incredible things that the human body can do.

The human body is like a vehicle. When you have a rare high-performance sports car, it's a real eye-catching talking point. It works the same with your body. If your own physical abilities are incredibly high-performing (like a sports car) then you'll be easily identifiable for those features. Maybe you're an Olympic rower. Maybe you've climbed Mount Everest. Maybe you've overcome a challenging physical situation. But it's your body, and your physical abilities, that make you unique.

A great example of this is Dan Thurman, past president of the National Speakers Association in America. Dan is a professional speaker and what sets him apart is the physical element he brings to his speeches. He does handstands on podiums to highlight the importance of balance.

He rides a two-metre tall unicycle to demonstrate the need to navigate change. And he even juggles sharp objects to illustrate the principles of performing under pressure. The things he can do with his body are what makes him stand out.

Turia Pitt is another great example. She was caught in – and survived – a fire in an ultra-marathon in Outback Australia. But it took immense fortitude, resilience and strength to come back from that injury, which, of course, still impacts her today. In Turia's situation she has both positive and negative body features that add to her uniqueness.

If your physicality is something that can highlight your uniqueness, fantastic. Maybe it's not just resilience and mindset, but something that has physically happened in your body, such as in the case of Turia Pitt. Or maybe your body is capable of doing something that most others can't. Sharing this widely might be the key to establishing your influence (presence) and, therefore, your uniqueness.

I love the quote from Simone Biles, who says, 'You all can judge my body all you want, but at the end of the day it's MY body. I love it and I'm comfortable in my own skin.'

When we create an exceptional brand, we create a space that highlights and inspires opportunities for people. Even if they aren't as physically strong or capable as you, your abilities inspire them. Your abilities help others to realise that they can be better and achieve their own potential. Then they start to focus on their own strengths and what they could do.

Of course, it doesn't necessarily mean that others will be inspired to climb Mount Everest or do things that maybe their bodies can't do. But you are reminding them that it's not just mindset that can set your brand apart. It's also about the physicality of your body.

Body Questions

1. Is there something that you have been able to physically do that others haven't?

2. Is there something that you can do that's so easy for you that you're often surprised that other people can't necessarily do that thing?

3. How do you do it, or how did you learn to do it?

4. What was the system and process that got you where you are and how can you use that to help others achieve their potential?

Remember, your physicality and your body can be a great inspiration for others to achieve their own potential.

Your Humour

For some their quick wit and humour can be the element of presence that makes them wildly unique. That's because humour makes others feel good and it helps you to be more interesting as well. There can be a lot of differences in humour – for example, you might use dry wit or a more literal humour – and your unique personality will enhance your own brand of humour.

Humour plays very well in the brand-building space because as humans we pay more attention to humorous things. And humour occurs in every society across the world – even in apes and rats.[40] It's a thing that brings us all together.

Humour is like adding colour to a painting, but it's adding colour to your communications. Working out your style of humour can be really valuable in your life generally, but also in creating an authentic and memorable brand.

Charlie Chaplin said, 'Through humour we see in what seems rational, the irrational; in what seems important, the unimportant.' It lightens our world, making hard things easier and impossible tasks possible. And when this is part of your brand you can be an important light-bringing influence on everyone around you.

Kate Burr, who is a comedian by trade, is also an expert in communicating with humour. She often talks about strategies to improve your humour and to identify what makes you funny. She also talks about a concept – funny in, funny out. In other words, you have to be consuming humorous content if you want to put out humorous content. So when you're using humour in your brand, you've got to find ways to bring in more humour and to find the humour style that suits you.

Another fantastic example of humour in a brand is Jeanne Robertson. Jeane is probably one of the most humorous business speakers in the world. She passed away just recently, but during her life she could tell a story on stage that would go on for 45 minutes. This seems like a very long time for an anecdote. But she had an immense understanding of humour. And the way she would explain the story, and the sheer number of laughs she would inspire throughout, was a testament to just how funny she was.

---

40 Sabato. G. 'What's So Funny? The Science of Why We Laugh'. 25 June 2019. Scientific American. Accessed at https://www.scientificamerican.com/article/ whats-so-funny-the-science-of-why-we-laugh/.

Humour isn't just fun, it also has great positive impacts. In fact, positive psychology studies show that humour correlates with wisdom, a love of learning, optimism and even well-being.[41] So when you display humour you're also conveying these excellent qualities to your listeners and that plays a strong role in building an authentic presence that conveys trust and influence.

Let's take a look at Seth Godin. If you ever get to see him speak on stage, he's incredibly insightful and very cerebral, captivating in terms of his insights and lightbulb moments. But he's not a particularly funny person. However, he still uses humour in his keynotes by bringing in funny images that demonstrate metaphors for what he's trying to say. So Seth is able to leverage humour through his metaphorical language and bring it into his communication. And that leads to an incredible impact – the kind we're all looking for in our own practice and brands.

Humour Questions

1. What type of humour is really authentic and congruent with who you are?

2. What would that humour look like if it was elevated?

3. What is the most extreme and funniest version of you, that can increase the humour and connection with your audience?

---

41 Peterson C, Ruch, W, Beermann, U, Park, N and Seligman, M. 'Strengths of character, orientations to happiness, and life satisfaction'. 21 June 2007. The Journal of Positive Psychology. Accessed at https://www.tandfonline.com/doi/abs/10.1080/17439760701228938.

Your Style

The next element that can drive your presence is your style. Your style is the way you do something. It is unique to you and sets you apart from the competition. When it comes to your brand, this is often a technical skill that you truly excel at.

Having a specific skill or version of doing something, provided it's effective and gets results, is a key differentiator in your brand. It sets you apart from others who do the same type of thing or work that you do, but which you just happen to do better or maybe differently.

Your unique skill is your brand's fingerprint. Everything you do within your brand carries that fingerprint which then becomes unequivocally associated with you, conveying your unique brand proposition to each person that comes into contact with your brand in any way. So whether that's your systems and processes, or writing books. Or maybe it's how you teach, or how you engage with your clients. Whatever it is, it's a unique skill that you have. And even when many, many other people do it, you happen to do it a bit differently.

Kelly Slater is perhaps the greatest athlete of all time, and certainly the world's best surfer. He's just turned 50 – half a century in real terms, but an eternity in the life of an elite athlete. Yet he continues to lead the world in surfing wins and will battle for his twelfth world title in 2022, three decades after his first pro competition.[42]

---

42 Feast, L. 'Kelly Slater at 50 waxes up for another world title battle'. 11 February 2022. Reuters. Accessed at https://www.reuters.com/lifestyle/sports/kelly-slater-50-waxes-up-another-world-title-battle-2022-02-11/#:~:text=Slater%20won%20world%20titles%20in,and%20Hawaii's%20John%20John%20Florence.

There's no doubt that Kelly is a champion and he has won each of these championships with a unique surfing style – one that sees him get incredible speed on the waves. He does this because he is a true technical surfing master – an expert at understanding waves and how best to work with wave motion.[43] In fact, in interviews he is reported as saying that you can't force turns in surfing in order to get up speed. You have to flow with the water. If you try to force against the water you're simply going to stop.[44]

For Kelly, his surfing is his unique style. He is always in flow and his style is designed to harness the energy of the wave in order to work with it, rather than fight against it. And that has seen him elevated to the top of his field and ensures that he is absolutely unique. There is no one like Kelly Slater.

Rachel Zoe, American fashion designer, businesswoman and author, says, 'Style is a way to say who you are without having to speak.' And this is true for Kelly Slater. I don't have to communicate with him. I don't have to talk to him. I can simply watch his style and learn a lot about him and his unique brand from that.

Becoming technically brilliant at something, in the way that Kelly Slater, and the other experts I mention in this chapter are, is not just a matter of luck. Research shows that these people generally possess the following qualities:

- knowledge – that makes them the most informed in their fields.

---

43 Hardacre, L. 'Breaking down Kelly Slater's Surfing'. 22 January 2022. Ombe.co. Accessed at https://www.ombe.co/guides/breaking-down-kelly-slaters-surfing.
44 Hardacre. 'Breaking down Kelly Slater's Surfing'.

- skill – that is both learned and influenced by natural talent and ability.

- achievement – far beyond what the average person will achieve.[45]

They reach these expert levels because they do things differently than others (with their own style) which allows them to elevate their knowledge, skill and achievement and bring those qualities into their brand.

More Than One Style for Success

Remember that as a leader it is up to you to cultivate and teach exceptionality in your team. But it's also important to remember that there is more than one way to achieve this.

For example, in my practice I am an expert at business books. And I often say there are writers who speak and speakers who write. And I am certainly the latter. So when I teach others to write books, I teach the way that I found works the fastest *for me* in order to get them started.

Of course, I fully expect them to hit walls, and it's at these walls that they begin learning about themselves and about the process that works best for them. And at that stage I can step back and let them lean into their own process for success.

Even though my personal technique works, it's based on a technical skill that I'm great at. While others might have their own areas of skill.

---

45 Cherry, K. 'How Hard Is It to Become an Expert.' 29 March 2022. Verywell Mind. Accessed at https://www.verywellmind.com/expertise-how-hard-is-it-to-become-an-expert-at-something-4173614.

It's important to remember that the style of your team might not be the same as yours. But if it works well, and gets results, that's OK too.

Style Questions

1. What is something that you excel in that you do in your own unique way?

2. Is this something that others struggle with?

3. Have you tried to do that thing in a normal way and not have it work as well as when you do it in your own unique way?

4. Have you tried to teach others this technique? Did they get the same results?

Your Communication

Communication is another area of skill that can truly set your brand apart. And it's a huge part of what makes up our presence and how we are viewed within the world. Yet we can often take our ability to communicate for granted. Because, let's face it, we do it every day.

But skilled professionals who are some of the best communicators in the world, don't just assume that length of time means they have all the skills they need. Instead, they understand how unique communication is and spend the time identifying their specific area of their communication skill. Then they work on amplifying that.

Maz Farrelly, media specialist, award-winning, international TV and film producer and author of *Engage-o-tainment*, is famous for saying, 'It is not my job to be interested – it is your job to be interesting.'

When this comes from Maz, we should take it seriously. She's a master communicator, who has worked for major media outlets, such as *BBC UK, ITV, Channel 4* and *Sky* in the UK, and the *ABC, Nine, Seven, Ten, Foxtel* and *BBC World Wide* in Australia. And she's been the power behind incredible shows such as *The X Factor, The Celebrity Apprentice* and *Q&A* (among many, many others!).

Maz has met thousands of possible candidates and talents for the shows she's worked on. She's listened to them sing, seen them dance and heard their stories and dreams. And she has an unerring ability to choose those people that are able to communicate to the world. Maz has been able to take these communication techniques and use them to inspire individuals and businesses to better create strategic goals, build staff engagement, have more engaged marketing and social media, become better negotiators and improve corporate culture. All because she has taught them how to be *better communicators*.

Tony Robbins writes in *Unlimited Power: The New Science of Personal Achievement*, 'Communication is power. Those who have mastered its effective use can change their own experience of the world and the world's experience of them. All behavior and feelings find their original roots in some form of communication. If you do what you've always done, you'll get what you've always gotten.'[46]

---

46 Robbins, T. (2008). Unlimited Power: The New Science Of Personal Achievement. Free Press.

Researchers define communication as 'the exchange of ideas and interaction among group members'.[47] It is the 'process of expressing ideas and feelings or of giving people information'. So people that are able to utilise communication techniques to do this well are the ones who become incredible contestants on the X Factor. Or they become powerfully effective CEOs or thought leaders.

But they don't do this by being vanilla, or by standing in the back of the room shouting to be overheard. They amplify their voice by leveraging the things that make them unique. And it's this uniqueness that acts as a megaphone to get them heard by more people, more often.

Finding Your Communication Style

Finding your unique communication style can help you to amplify your communication. And sometimes it's helpful to think of these styles as the four Arisotelian elements: earth, water, fire and air.

---

47 Fatimayin, F. 'What is Communication?' October 2018. Accessed at https://www. researchgate.net/publication/337649561_What_is_Communication.

Aristotelian elements

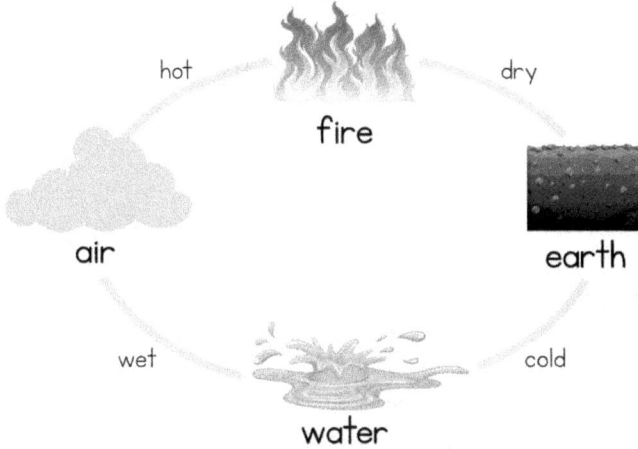

Fire

People who have a high amount of fire in their communication style tend to have an emotional response to situations. They are quick to make decisions but can be seen as uncaring. They often focus on the outcome over anything else.

Water

People who have a high amount of water in their communication style are much more aware of other people – their values, feelings and the things that concern them. Like water they tend to take on the feelings of others around them. They want everyone to be in harmony in order to communicate well and resolve conflict. They are often seen as soft and emotional.

Earth

People with a high proportion of earth in their communication tend to focus on specifics, such as details and plans, and they want to communicate (and receive communication) in an organised, step-by-step way. They are logical and influenced by data, facts and figures. They make decisions slowly and need to trust the other person before doing so.

Air

People with a high proportion of air in their communication style are very ideas oriented. They have the ability to bring disparate ideas (and disparate idea makers) together for even better results. But they are often seen as unrealistic dreamers. These people are 'big picture' communicators and don't like to focus on the minutiae that drives other decision makers.

Examples

Nick Cummins, The Honey Badger – Earth

Steve Irwin, The Crocodile Hunter – Earth/Fire

Rebel Wilson – Air

Magda Zubankski – Air

Paul Hogan – Earth

Turia Pitt – Earth

Germain Greer – Air/Fire

Celeste Barber – Earth

Elle McPherson – Air

Your Unique Combination

Each person's communication style will be a combination of the above – and yours will be too. And even though your communication style is different from many of the other people that you'll be communicating with, you can learn to communicate with every other type of communicator, particularly once you understand the different styles.

However, one of the most common mistakes that people make in their communication is believing that everyone sees the world in the same way that they do. But it's actually unlikely that the person that you're communicating with has the same communication style that you do. And when your message is complicated or perhaps a little bit difficult, having a different communication style can lead to conflict.

However, you can avoid those conflicts if you simply understand your own communication style, as well as the different styles that other people may have. This allows you to highlight your natural strengths in your own communication and create your own unique communication style that avoids misunderstanding and conflict.

Using Your Uniqueness to Amplify Your Communication

Whenever I work with a speaker preparing them to take the stage, one of the first things we do is identify what it is that makes them unique – the thing that makes them *interesting* as Maz would say. We find this thing and then we amplify it. And this is precisely what Maz does when she chooses the participants on her shows.

Before you can amplify your own communication and communication techniques, you need to determine what makes you unique. Take the following four steps:

Step 1: Start by **identifying your values.** Find them and share them.

Step 2: Next, consider your communication techniques. You should always speak your mind and **be honest and upfront.**

Step 3: Third, get inside the mind of your audience. **Knowing your audience** will help you express yourself in a way they'll understand.

Step 4: Fourth, **package your messages.** Know your **communication style** and use it to deliver your messages.

Communication Questions

1. What is your communication style? Are you air and fire, or maybe primarily water?

2. How does your communication style impact how you connect with your audience?

3. What can you do to amplify this communication?

How to Bring Out the Best in Others

When you have presence you have the ability to influence people. They feel they know you and trust you, and that makes them amenable to your guidance. But that influence also means that you have a responsibility to bring out the best in others.

So, how do you bring the best out in others? Or, another way to ask this is, how do you lead? Your ability to bring out the best in others and lead people could be the unique thing that sets you apart and creates that space that you can occupy above your competitors.

So what is it that elevates you to the level of exceptional in your leadership of others? Maybe you're encouraging. Maybe you're good at delegating. Or maybe you're a great coach.

Whatever it is, the ability to lead is a unique skill. And a lot of people who have this skill don't see it in themselves. For them it might be an innate trait or something that comes easily to them. And because of that they don't necessarily value it. This can be especially true for women.

Being able to lead and bring out the best in people is a little bit like being a navigator in a rally car. You aren't driving the car yourself. Instead, your job is to put the person in the driver's seat and support them along that way.

As Lao Tzu said, 'A leader is best when people barely know he exists, when his work is done, his aim fulfilled, they will say: we did it ourselves.' The best leaders innately know (or learn) that it's not about them. It's their ability to make other people shine that is their true power and the thing that gives them their real presence.

Throughout my career I've known some great leaders who have had the skill to bring out the best in others. My previous boss, Tracey Mathers, is one of the first that comes to mind. As I mentioned earlier in this book, she comes from the family of Sir Robert Mathers, who owned a chain of shoe stores in Australia. I worked under Tracey and with the family for 15 years and in the end they were like my own family.

Working under Tracey was a wonderful experience. She is an incredibly encouraging person, and she helps a lot of women to feel better about themselves by empowering them to be the best they can be.

As an employee at their store, I have certainly felt that myself. She constantly gives people compliments to motivate and inspire them. She seems to recognise that people are quite hard on themselves and she gives them the boost they need to see the best in themselves. She certainly had that special leadership skill that gave her influence – in the best way – on others.

According to Seek.com, a market leader in online employment marketplaces, the number one reason that people leave their jobs is due to poor management. But a leader with the kind of unique presence and ability to build others up and make them shine is absolutely rare and wonderful. And it's the scarcity of this skill that – if you have it – allows you to create a wildly unique brand.

Questions for How to Bring Out the Best in Others

1. What type of leader are you known for being? Are you known as being an empowering leader, an insightful leader, an encouraging leader or a resilient leader?

2. If you were to ever write a book about leadership, what type of leader would it be about? What category might it sit in?

3. How do you do your version of leadership? If you had to step outside yourself and unpack a map of how you lead, what would that look like?

Embracing Your Uniqueness for Exceptionality

Each of these elements – your experiences, your mindset and your presence (together and in combination) – can be used to develop your uniqueness and elevate your brand. And within each of the broad categories there are many different ways to embrace them and showcase who you are. I'd also bet that you have one of these in your practice already – if you could just recognise it.

Take a little while and consider – which are you already using? And which additional element might you be able to embrace to demonstrate how you are wildly unique and, ultimately, grow your exceptionality?

Section 3

World Class

'Everything can be improved.'

– Clarence W. Barron

Overview

What Does Being 'World Class' Mean?

World class means 'being of the highest calibre in the world'.[48] What a fantastic definition. Because being of the highest calibre in the world is precisely what we need to be if we want to truly be considered exceptional.

But knowing that we want to be exceptional – or world class – is not enough. What's most important is knowing how to get there. And in order to become world class you must be continuously improving.

What is Continuous Improvement?

The idea of continuous improvement is not one that's often talked about in the thought leader, consultant or expert industries, even though it's a highly developed part of the corporate industry. In fact, the idea of a continuous improvement process within the corporate arena was originally developed as a management methodology by Toyota in Japan.[49]

---

48 'world-class.' Merriam-Webster Dictionary, Merriam-Webster, Incorporated, 2022. Accessed at https://www.merriam-webster.com/dictionary/world-class#:~:text=%3A%20being%20of%20the%20highest%20caliber,world%20a%20world%2Dclass%20athlete.

49 'What is *kaizen* and how does Toyota use it?' 31 May 2013. Toyota UK Magazine. Accessed at https://mag.toyota.co.uk/kaizen-toyota-production-system/.

Knowing that we want to be exceptional – or world class – is not enough. What's most important is knowing how to get there. And in order to become world class you must be continuously improving.

Known as *kaizen*, it is one of the core principles of The Toyota Production System. In essence, kaizen is the 'quest for continuous improvement'.[50] In practice, it's about making incremental improvements over time, as opposed to big breakthrough moments. It allows you to streamline work and reduce waste no matter what your business is without having to rely on moments of brilliance or inspiration. In some ways it's like an elite athlete who simply practices and practices and practices, rather than one who relies solely on their talent.

Why Continuous Improvement Matters for Exceptionality

Winston Churchill once said, 'To improve is to change; to be perfect is to change often.' It sounds obvious, but many times we feel – both consciously and subconsciously – like only the naturally gifted get to be exceptional. Whereas the truth is that exceptional people don't actually focus on *being exceptional*. Because being exceptional isn't the end goal. In fact, there is no end goal. Exceptional people simply focus on getting a little bit better that day. And then the next. And then the next.

It's a little bit like being on a treadmill on an incline. There's no end goal per se. You're just focussing on putting one foot in front of the other again and again, as you continue to rise up, to elevate, even if it's only 1% at a time. Over time, you will end up climbing higher than you ever thought possible.

But as much as growing and developing matters for an individual to achieve a level of exceptionality, it's also important for our day-to-day happiness at work.

---

50 'What is *kaizen*'.

Exceptional people don't actually focus on being exceptional. Because being exceptional isn't the end goal. In fact, there is no end goal. Exceptional people simply focus on getting a little bit better that day. And then the next. And then the next.

Happiness At Work

Dr Jess Pryce-Jones wrote the book *Happiness at Work: Maximizing Your Psychological Capital*[51]. In her research she found that the happier people were at work, the more engagement was built within the organisation.[52] In other words, happy workers were better workers overall.

Of course, she then needed to determine what created happiness at work. And what she identified in her research is that people were happy at work when they could get through the highs and the lows while still feeling like they were achieving their potential and growing into even greater potential.[53] So the key aspect to feeling happy at work for you and your team is that they are achieving *and* growing.

The Structure of Happiness at Work – The 5 Cs

Dr Pryce Jones' research found five areas that help people feel like they're achieving their potential at work:

1. Commitment

2. Confidence

3. Contribution

4. Conviction

5. Culture[54]

---

51 Pryce-Jones, J. (2010). Happiness at Work: Maximizing Your Psychological Capital for Success. Wiley.

52 Pryce-Jones. Happiness at Work.

53 Pryce-Jones. Happiness at Work.

54 Pryce-Jones. Happiness at Work.

Together these '5 Cs' are a powerful methodology that fast-tracks change and growth at the individual, team and organisational levels.

The 5 Cs Model

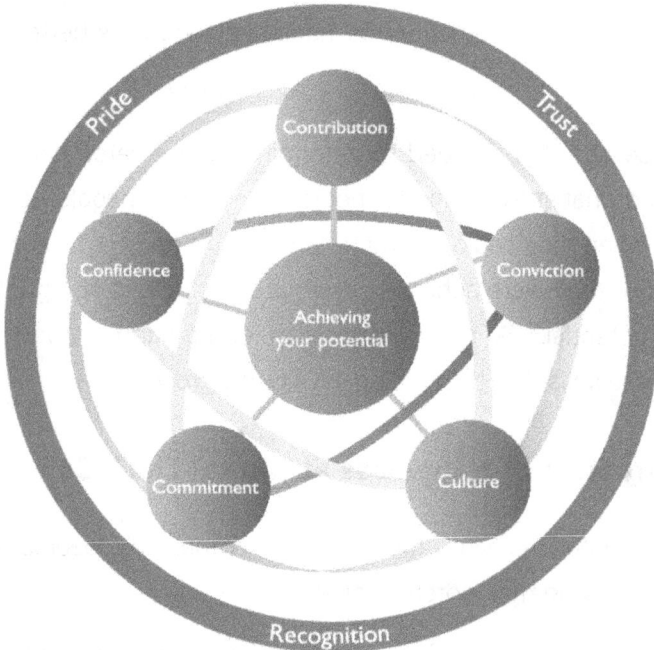

Taking The First Step Towards Continuous Improvement

I spent many years as a productivity consultant. And during that time, I found that while most organisations have at least some focus on progress, most people at an individual level are not actually that focused on continuous improvement. Instead, they're constantly on the back foot, managing the day-to-day tasks and putting out fires. So they never make the time to stop to make the system better. That forces them to continue treading water just to keep afloat rather than progressing.

The biggest issue, however, is that most of the time, they aren't working on the problem once the fire is out either. In fact, it generally isn't until I ask the question – how will you stop this happening again – that they actually stop to work out how to fix it for good. But once they do that, they're on the road to improvement.

The Virgin Australia Example – Plan, Check, Deliver, Debrief and Improve

Having worked with over 27 different industries in implementing productivity, processes and systems, there's one industry that always stands out to me as an excellent example of the continuous improvement process – airlines. When I worked with Virgin Australia, I worked closely with the head of flight operations and his team, who were all senior pilots. They had an excellent strategy for ensuring they were continuously improving – plan, check, deliver, debrief and improve.

The Power of Continuous Improvement in Your Consulting Practice

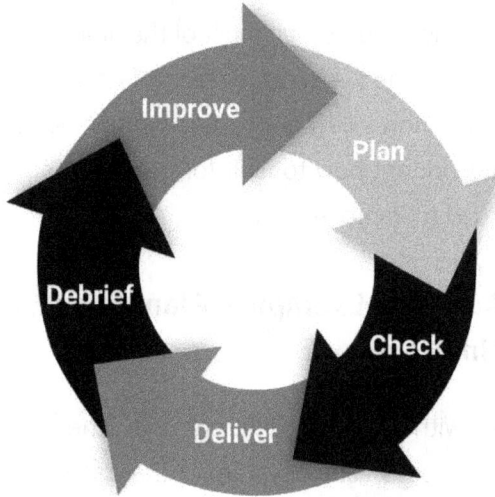

After identifying the actual goal of the particular program or process, Virgin's first step would be to plan for the steps that they would need to follow in order to deliver the results. Next, they would check the process to ensure its efficacy before moving onto their delivery of the process. This was helped by their obsession with checklists. They had checklists for checklists and they followed every single thing on that list in order to make sure that the process would run absolutely smoothly, with no errors, and that every step was captured and accomplished.

Once they delivered a particular process, they didn't just high five and start again. They took the time to debrief. They came back together, discussed how it went, what worked and what didn't and, importantly, what they needed to update for next time.

Did the process need work? If it did, what was the problem? Was it the templates? Was it a certain step? They identified the areas that needed improvements and then they implemented those improvements. And then they started the cycle again.

Implementing the Virgin Approach

The Virgin approach, and the idea of *kaizen* or continuous improvement generally, is something that we can, and should be, implementing in our own practices. Of course, if we're still in the process of building our practices, this can look a little bit different. After all, Virgin and Toyota are both established businesses. So, when they make improvements, they are doing so on firmly established practices. On the other hand, when we're building a practice, there can be a lot of pressure because we're creating a process for things that aren't yet in existence.

Even so, using the tool of continuous improvement can help you get there. You make your plan, you deliver, you debrief and then you improve. Constantly checking and improving and then repeating the cycle will help you both build out your practice and improve those processes as you go.

Improving is Better than Perfection

As the famous American author Mark Twain said, 'Continuous improvement is better than delayed perfection.' Many of us delay our processes and delivery or stop trying to execute our plans simply because they're not yet perfect. But in order to become perfect – or better yet, in order to become *exceptional* – we need to become those people who obsess about our continuous improvement process. We need to stop getting bogged down in blocks or in things that are holding us back from progressing.

David Shenk, author of *The Genius in All of Us*, describes the human phenomenon where we believe that people who are geniuses at what they do must have an innate talent or ability that allows them to achieve that level of exceptionality.[55] In other words, they are exceptional because they're built that way. But that is not always the case. We *all* have the potential to be a genius at what we do, as long as we are focused on being better every day.

Mindset, Momentum, Motivation

In order to embrace our own potential to achieve exceptionality through continuous improvement we have to embrace three important elements:

1. Mindset

2. Momentum

3. Motivation

In the next three chapters we'll focus on these three elements and how they support our task of continuous improvement and help us rise to a genius, or exceptional, level (and to keep going from there!).

---

55 Shenk, D. (2011). The Genius in All of Us: New Insights into Genetics, Talent, and IQ. Random House USA Inc..

Continuous Improvement Overview Questions

As you go through this final section, consider the following questions:

1. How important is growth to you?

2. Do you value getting better? And if you don't, then what impact is that having on you? Do you feel depressed? Do you feel like you're not getting anywhere? Do you feel like you're going backwards? Do you feel like nothing's working?

3. What do you do to try to get better at your job or within your expertise?

If you can work out where you want to get better, you will become exceptional.

Chapter 8

World Class Mindset

John Bertrand is an Australian yachtsman who is best known for skippering the Australia II to victory in the 1983 America's Cup.[56] In fact, this was a momentous day in boating (and sporting) history – particularly for Australia – because it ended 132 years of American supremacy in the America's Cup. However, it wasn't the first time Bertrand and his team had competed in that race. In fact, he had participated three times before his famous win in 1983 (1970, 1974 and 1980).

So what changed? Famously, it was Bertrand and the team's mindset.[57] Bertrand realised that they weren't the inferior crew and they didn't have an inferior boat. But what they did have was an inferior mindset. They didn't believe they were world class. They didn't believe they had the ability to compete on this stage. And they simply didn't believe they could beat the Americans.

So, they shifted their mindset. They worked hard to *believe* they belonged on the world stage. They stopped referring to the American team by name, and just started calling them 'the red boat'. This helped

---

56 Sport Australia Hall of Fame. 'John Bertrand AO, Sailing'. Accessed at https://sahof.org.au/hall-of-fame-member/john-bertrand/#:~:text=A%20world%20champion%20and%20Olympic,Montreal%20in%20the%20Finn%20Class.

57 Bertrand, J. (1985). Born to win: a lifelong struggle to capture the America's Cup (as told to Patrick Robinson). Sydney: Bantam Books.

remove some of that cache. And then they focused on their own training, their own team and their own boat. And, ultimately, their mindset work led to the amazing 1983 win that changed the way the world viewed Australian yachtsmen.

When it comes to building our own world class brand it also all starts with our *mindset*. So, if you truly want your practice to become exceptional, if you truly want to continue to improve all the time, you need to prioritise your mindset development.

And when it comes to being world class, it starts with understanding that it is not the same as being perfect.

Exceptional People Are Authentic

If I could leave you with any message about becoming world class it's *don't try to be perfect*. You're not striving for absolute perfection. It's far more about progress than perfection, and a commitment to excellence (or a commitment to continually trying to be better) is all that's needed.

If you do find yourself falling into the trap of striving for perfection it can feel like slipping into quicksand. You're trying to move forward to free yourself, but you're stuck and can't move. And that's the problem with perfection. The act of reaching out for perfection actually stops you from moving. It freezes you in place so that you're unable to take a chance on anything or take any new steps for fear of falling short of that ultimate goal. And that means that no change can happen.

If I could leave you with any message about becoming world class it's don't try to be perfect. You're not striving for absolute perfection. It's far more about progress than perfection, and a commitment to excellence (or a commitment to continually trying to be better) is all that's needed.

On the other hand, if you can create a brand that's wildly unique and world class then people will want to emulate that. When you focus more on your progress, and on being authentic (rather than being perfect), your audience will see that. Your authentic communications will show them that you're working hard to improve day in and day out, and they'll be able to see the massive growth that you make.

In fact, research shows that within organisations authentic leadership reinforces the emotional connection of workers to those organisations.[58] And this increases their commitment and creativity and improves their job performance.

In the same way, once your audience sees your own progress and growth, they'll feel more connected to you and committed to your brand. They'll want to emulate you and will begin to embrace the possibility that they could do it themselves because *they'll actually see themselves in the process.* That inspires them and motivates them to begin to make some changes.

Brene Brown said, 'Yes, I am imperfect and vulnerable and sometimes afraid, but that doesn't change the truth that I am also brave and worthy of love and belonging.'

---

58 Duarte, A, Ribeiro, N, Semedo, A and Gomes, D. Authentic Leadership and Improved Individual Performance: Affective Commitment and Individual Creativity's Sequential Mediation. 7 May 2021. Frontiers in Psychology. Accessed at https://www.frontiersin.org/articles/10.3389/fpsyg.2021.675749/full.

Authenticity Questions

1. Who is someone you really admire and would love to emulate?

2. Ask them about their biggest mistakes. And if you don't know them, research them. Google their name and the word mistakes. What have you learned? What are the chinks in their armour?

3. Do you have similar chinks in your armour that could help you to feel more connected, more human and more inspiring to your own audience and, as you demonstrate your own growth on the path to continuous improvement, really help you to emulate an exceptional personal brand?

Exceptional People Have Curiosity

When it comes to being exceptional, it's often our own egos that hold us back. For example, when we have our egos at play, it can stop us from being vulnerable enough to ask our customers what they need. And it can stop us from recognising and making the daily changes that we need to continuously improve, grow and become exceptional.

Exceptional people are growth-driven. They're open to ideas, people and experiences. They understand themselves enough and are comfortable enough with who they are, that they're willing to ask questions and not feel like they have to know everything. The benefit of curiosity is that you gain insight and empathy, and you remove assumptions that may not necessarily be true allowing you to be more customer centric.

In fact, this curiosity means that you actually become more credible because you know more, and people trust that when you *say* you know something, you actually do.

What stops us from being growth driven is our vulnerability. It's the fear of looking like we don't know what we're doing or that we're going to look stupid. But what we have to really do is be present and really listen to what our customers are saying. It's like opening a door to another world because it helps you know what you don't know.

If you don't ask your customers what it is that they need help with, you can't help them. On the other hand, when you do ask them for their input or insight into something, they feel valued.

I was recently speaking with a gentleman about helping with some sales content for his cycling tour business. I asked him why he wanted to look at content creation – specifically his newsletters. He said that he had been really struggling with what to put out in his newsletters and how to engage with his audience.

The more I spoke with him and listened to what his challenges were, the more I realised that his biggest problem was that he really didn't know what his customers wanted. My worry was that if I was to do the work for him, it might not result in growing his business in exactly the way he wanted. It was a real gamble.

So, I asked him, 'What is it that your customers want?' He said, 'Well, I think they want this. I think they want that. I think they need these photos. I think they need me to write about this.' I said, 'Well, the problem is that you're making a lot of assumptions. You're thinking about what *you* think they need, but you haven't actually asked them what *they* think they need.'

I asked him when he had last surveyed his customers because his open rates were really quite high with his communications, but no one was buying. His response was that he had never asked them. When I asked him why not, he said, 'Well, isn't that my job to know what they need?' I agreed, but I also explained that we've just come through a pandemic. And whenever you're in a disrupted market, people's needs can change. Now, we don't know what they need. Or, if we have any idea, we need to recognise that it may or may not actually be true.

I shared with him that when COVID hit I began to question my clients' biggest concerns in my own practice. I was talking to a lot of clients, and whilst they would tell me things that were challenging and worrying, I wasn't quite sure if there was a pattern, or if it was just my perspective.

I'm a marketer. I do sales training as well, but my real forte is marketing. Like many people at the beginning of COVID, I lost a lot of my own clients. But rather than sit back and guess the motivation, I went out and asked them, 'What do you need? What's the biggest problem that you've got at the moment?'

Interestingly, they all said sales. Of course, I pointed out that there are other specialised salespeople who could train and teach them, but that I was happy to do it if that's what they wanted. I asked, 'Do you want me to teach you? Because there's other people who can do that.' They said, 'No, we like your approach to selling.'

Asking led to a lightbulb moment in my own business. Because I was so close to my own stuff, I never really looked at myself as a salesperson. And I'd never really offered my clients a good look at my unique sales processes. But my clients had seen me as a salesperson and they wanted to know how I did my own sales work. And so when I took the time to *ask* them what they needed I was then able to give that to them.

Of course it wasn't as simple as just telling them what I do. I had to really think about how I sell and what makes me unique. What's the unique skill that they are wanting to learn? And as I explored that aspect of my work I realised that it was really about the style of selling that I utilise – what I call soft selling.

Soft selling is a type of selling that is subtle but effective and impactful. It's focused on being helpful, not aggressive. So rather than trying to talk people into buying things, we're selling help or solutions.

I worked with a lady who was struggling in her business. We looked at some emerging trends and found that retreats were becoming an important area in her business.

I asked her, 'Have you considered putting on a retreat for your clients?' She said no. She was concerned that if she booked the venue, and then no one wanted to come, that she'd then be on the hook for cancellation fees. I agreed that it was a risk, but also that the thing she needed to do to minimise her risk was just to ask her clients.

I said, 'Go out and ask your clients if they'd like to attend a retreat. Once you've conducted an expression of interest, then you can make an educated deduction about whether the retreat is a goer or not based on the evidence that you're seeing.' She had never thought about it like that.

Curiosity in your practice means going out and asking your clients what they need or want. It means gaining expressions of interest, and finding out what they need the most help with.

Sir Ken Robinson, British author, speaker and international advisor on education, said, 'Curiosity is the engine of achievement.' You can only achieve progress, and therefore excellence and a world-class brand, if you include curiosity as part of your practice DNA. It needs to be part of your processes and systems for growing your business and your brand.

Curiosity Questions

1. When was the last time you asked your clients (or team) what they're struggling with or what they need from you?

2. How does this align with what you think they needed from you or were struggling with?

3. How do you need to change your approach now that you know what they really need from you?

If you can answer these questions, and make any required changes, then you're going to be on the track to exceptionality.

Exceptional People Are Courageous

We all face times in our lives when we're unsure of doing something. Maybe we've never done it before. Or maybe we're afraid of making a mistake. Exceptional people understand they're going to have to do things outside of their comfort zone. They understand it takes courage. And even those who are experienced and confident still face times where they are stretched and face fear. This could be the fear of losing clients or the fear of not being liked. It might be the fear of losing money, the fear of losing market share or even the fear of losing team members.

But when people are courageous it's like putting armour on. They're finding a way to feel strong going in, so they can face those things that they haven't been able to before. For each person, the methods they use to find this courage will be different. But it's a vital part of becoming exceptional.

My Great Aunt Lillian May Armfield is a heroine of mine. She was Australia's first police woman, hired onto the Sydney police force in 1915, and she spent over 30 years working and, ultimately, leading the N.S.W Policewomen. Of course, it wasn't easy.

Aunt Lilly wasn't permitted to wear a uniform or carry a weapon (until much later in her career). She didn't have her medical costs covered when she was injured on the job, or accrue superannuation like her male counterparts. And she worked in some of the worst slums in Sydney, notoriously fighting against the infamous 'razor gang' violence of the 1920s. Yet, through it all, she remained courageously focused on her work helping women who were caught up in the dark underbelly of Sydney to escape to a better life.

In fact, she was such an iconic heroine that she was featured on the show *Underbelly*. But she died poor, and lived with very little recognition of the amazing work that she was doing. However, she never let that stop her. She knew her purpose in life – her truth was saving girls – and she woke up every day and courageously focused on achieving that purpose, no matter how difficult it was.

Most of us aren't facing razor-wielding gangs, but being courageous is just as important in our careers as it was for my Aunt Lilly, especially when we're on the road to becoming world class brands and exceptional leaders.

Experts believe that courageous leadership is summed up by courageous action.[59] To take courageous actions you need to 'model the way and create the path. Reflect on why you want to be a leader and what you bring to your organization and profession. Seek feedback and make course corrections. Keep the gap between who you show up as and who you want to be small. Develop a reputation for being helpful and in the service of your organisation [or practice]. Create transparency, nurture trust and explicitly and intentionally practice inclusivity. Remove the fences in your process. Start with small opportunities and grow.'[60]

As courageous leaders on the road to exceptionality we need to remember that as Anaïs Nin said, 'Life shrinks or expands in proportion to one's courage.' We need to be ready to expand our lives – and our practices – by embracing courage and utilising courageous action in our leadership.

Courageous Leadership Questions

1. What are you most afraid of doing that would give you growth in your business or your brand? Would it be around increasing your pricing? Or offering a new or different service?

2. Who do you know that could advise you and help you to put on your courageous armour, overcome your fears and take those next steps?

---

59 Jones, D and Davis, S. (2020). Courageous Leadership: Walking Your Talk from Wherever You Are. The Serials Librarian. Accessed at https://www.tandfonline.com/doi/full/10.1080/0361526X.2020.1744410.

60 Jones. Courageous Leadership.

Exceptional People Value Connections

When it comes to becoming world class, connection isn't just about networks or your little black book. When people feel like they connect with you at a human level, they feel safe, that they belong and that they can be themselves, both vulnerable and brave. Every human wants to achieve their potential and to grow into being the best version of themselves. And being connected at a human level helps them to achieve that.

Connection is like a warm blanket. It feels safe. It feels cosy. And when people feel connected they feel like everything is going to be OK. Researcher Amy Cuddy and consultants Matthew Kohut and John Neffinger out of Harvard Business School demonstrate that just like hiding under the blankets as a child helped you to feel safe, connection also creates a sense of psychological safety.[61]

Their argument is that leaders who begin by establishing trust through warmth and understanding – rather than emphasising competence and credentials – facilitate 'both the exchange and acceptance of ideas' so 'people really hear [the] message and become open to it'.[62] In other words, when people feel like they are connected and belong, they're more willing to try new things – including things that will help them to improve.

Tom Ford, the American fashion designer said, 'The most important things in life are the connections you make with others.' This is

---

61 Cuddy, A, Kohut, M and Neffinger, J. (2013). Connect, Then Lead. Harvard Business Review. Accessed at https://hbr.org/2013/07/connect-then-lead.
62 Cuddy. Connect, Then Lead.

something that really exceptional people – such as Tom Ford – have as part of their brand and their focus.

Take, for example, Princess Diana. She had this incredible connection with people. She would go out and visit homeless people, people who were sick, people who had HIV and AIDS even at a time when fear was rife around these situations and illnesses. Even more, she physically connected with them.

For Princess Diana this became part of her 'brand' – of what she was known for. It was a symbolic way of dealing with the media as well and sending the message about the power of connection. She was in the royal family, which was very staid, and very formal and not seen as warm or understanding. But because she was such a strong connector, she was able to change that opinion, certainly for herself and her children. And that's shown through the legacy that she's left.

Another exceptional person is Roger Federer. He has a warmth about him, even though he's a high-performing tennis player and ruthless on a tennis court. But he's a true connector in terms of how he engages at a human level. He's warm, funny, self-deprecating and very likable. And as a result, he's considered to be an exceptional human being, not just an exceptional tennis player.

Connection Questions

1. Do you consider yourself a people person? To what extent do you feel like you connect with people or do you feel like you don't?

2. How do you bring warmth and connection into your interactions with others? What do you do to help

people feel safe? Is it that you call people by their name? Or maybe you're friendly, funny or smile often? Or maybe you're warm and great at making eye contact?

Exceptional People Have Standards

All exceptional people have standards because having standards means having a benchmark of expectations. Without standards, there's no way to continuously improve. Or more accurately, no way of judging that you have improved.

But having standards – having a level of expectations – means that you first and foremost have an awareness of a standard that you need to reach, and, secondly, that you can focus on not just achieving the standard but on raising the standard through your efforts at improvement.

Understanding the standard you need to reach is the first goal. When we were looking to get our first bulldog, we started to look for a breeder. First of all, we wanted to make sure we found an ethical breeder. We didn't want someone who was breeding a brachycephalic dog that would knowingly have breathing issues. And we thought that might be impossible. But if it had turned out to be impossible to buy from an ethical breeder we were prepared not to buy an English bulldog. We were determined that we would find a breeder who was adhering to the standards or looking to improve the standards of the breed.

After lots of research we were ultimately referred to a breeder on the Sunshine Coast. Not only did she have pure grade champion dogs, but she was very particular in how she bred each and every puppy. Her goal was to improve the standards of the breed, so that it didn't have breathing issues. And because of that focus, she's built a reputation for being a breeder who is ethical.

When it comes to your brand, it's the same thing. You need to decide what standard you're going to reach for. Because if you don't have a standard for yourself and for your expectations of others, then you simply won't strive to improve, to grow and to become exceptional. As the proverb goes – 'If you don't stand for something, you'll fall for anything.'

Whether you're a dog breeder or a marketer or have another niche entirely, striving for high standards matters. This is demonstrated by the fact that researchers across almost every industry in the world consistently focus on finding and expanding on the 'best practice standards' for their industry. In one set of research for Australian teachers, researchers found that carefully prepared and valid standards give leaders a clear direction on how to plan their own professional learning and provide challenging goals to aim for over time.[63] And it's these standards and challenges that allow you to strive for continuous improvement and to ultimately become world class.

This was demonstrated very well by one of my fantastic clients, Sarah. When Sarah came to work with me, she had just started her business and her revenue at the time was at about $40,000 per year. She knew what she wanted to do to grow the business – and that was to take it into a consulting practice – but she wasn't a hundred percent sure

---

63 Ingvarson, L and Anderson, M. (2007). Standards for Leadership: Gateway to a Stronger Profession? Qualitative Social Research. Accessed at https://www. researchgate.net/publication/41154599_Standards_for_Leadership_Gateway_ to_a_Stronger_Profession.

whether her idea would work. She also wasn't sure how to set pricing, what clients to target or whether clients would actually want to work with her. All she did know was that she had been working with accountants and chief financial officers and she really liked helping these people.

Sarah felt that she understood their world and she understood what they were trying to do because that was her background as well. So, she had the credibility, she had the experience, she even had the right target clients. But her business still wasn't growing. And that's because she didn't have any benchmarks. She didn't have any standards to work towards. Even her expectations were quite low.

What we had to do was reset her standards of what was possible so she had something to strive for and achieve. We started with small standards and then we began to gradually build up on that approach to where she ultimately needed her standards to be. And it worked. Within about 12 months, she was turning over a million dollars a year and she is well and truly on her way to creating a very successful practice.

Standards Questions

1. Do you have an awareness of the standard that you are trying to achieve? For example, if you want to be able to speak at conferences and on stages, then what is the standard of professionalism and behaviour? Are you a $10,000 speaker versus a $50,000 speaker versus a $100,000 speaker? What are the standards that are expected at each of those levels?

2. Is there a standard that you are aware of? If there is, can you identify exactly what is it? What are the behavioural indicators? The financial indicators?

3. Once you understand the standard, what do you need to work towards it? You should be focusing every day on being 1% better and moving towards that standard.

4. Are you surrounding yourself with people who will hold you to that higher standard? If not, why not? And how can you remedy that?

Conclusion

Authenticity, curiosity, courageousness, connection and striving for high standards – these are all elements of the mindset that you need in order to embrace the idea of *kaizen* or continuous improvement. And embracing this continuous improvement will set you on the right track to leaving average, 'good enough' attitudes behind and becoming truly world class. Of course, once you get started on the right track you still need the engine to keep you going. And that is momentum.

Chapter 9

World Class Momentum

Achieving momentum is a vital element in achieving a world class practice. Without momentum you won't have the impetus to keep challenging yourself, improving and growing. You won't have the constant force needed to keep you in motion despite difficulties and setbacks (of which there are bound to be some). And you simply won't have the engine to drive forward towards exceptionality.

So, how do you develop world class momentum? By establishing cadence, setting big goals, creating and making mistakes and making consistent efforts over the long term.

Cadence

When it comes to your business or practice, your cadence is how often something happens. But the better definition is a rhythmic sequence for managing a task. So the better your cadence, the more seamless and smoothly your practice will run.

I mentioned Sarah in the last chapter. When she came to work with me, she was obsessed about her cadence and systems. Unfortunately, she just didn't have a lot in place to grow her business. The good news was that she was already exceptional at what she did. She just needed the systems and routines in her practice to take that exceptionality and extrapolate it across a wider audience.

So together we put in the routines that she needed to do every day, week, month and year. And we set up particular projects as well to ensure that she had the systems in place to support those projects. But the thing that really shifted her practice was when she was able to get her team into the cadence and rhythm of the systems. Once she had her team in place and in flow, she was in an excellent place to really grow her business. And it was then that we were able to take her $40,000 a year business and within 18 months, turn it into a $750,000 a year business.

The truly exceptional really obsess over their routines. They know that if they can get these in place, everything takes a lot less effort, and they'll have more flow in their business and in their lives. And then they are far less likely to fail and have to keep starting all over again.

James Clear in his book, *Atomic Habits,* talks about his journey of recovering from an injury and some of the things that he had to do each day, week, month and year to get his health back on track.[64] He said of that experience, 'I began to realize that my results had very little to do with the goals I set and nearly everything to do with the systems that I followed.'[65]

James also posits that we rise to the level of our goals, but we fall to the level of our systems.[66] And I totally agree with this. In my time as a productivity consultant the biggest thing that was often missing for

---

64 Clear, J. (2018). Atomic Habits: An Easy & Proven Way to Build Good Habits & Break Bad Ones. Avery.
65 Clear. Atomic Habits.
66 Clear. Atomic Habits.

people in terms of being able to get control of their work and improve their productivity was systems, habits and routines. They simply didn't have them in place.

If you're in this situation then you're constantly in chaos reactivity. You'll be dealing with multiple demands and struggling to say no to a lot of things. Getting out of that place and into a smooth cadence is important, but you don't have to do everything in a single day. Instead, we need to be focusing on the continuous improvement of our systems and processes as well as our overall brand.

Continuous Improvement Of Our Cadence

In *Atomic Habits*, James talks about the power of tiny habits to become 1% better every day.[67] Robin Sharma, one of the world's leading leadership experts, agrees with this approach as well. In his book, *The 5am Club*, he talks about habits and routines. He focuses on getting in control of your morning and elevating your life as a result.[68] And for him it's about grabbing that 1% of each day that will allow you to ultimately gain maximum autonomy and control over your life.[69]

In the *5am Club*, Sharma recommends including a certain set of routines – move, reflect, grow.[70] This not only sets you up well physically and mentally for the day ahead, but it also gives you an opportunity to focus on the growth element in your life or business. But whatever routines you put into place, if they are systemised and designed to give you momentum in your life and career, that's a great thing.

---

67 Clear, J. Atomic Habits.

68 Sharma, R. (2018). The 5am Club: Own Your Morning. Elevate Your Life. HarperCollins Publishers.

69 Sharma. The 5am Club.

70 Sharma,. The 5am Club.

Research shows that tiny habits can lead to big changes.[71] In fact 20% of people that begin to implement tiny habits in their lives see major changes to their cadence within less than a week.[72] They are able to do more, achieve more, take on more challenges and strive towards becoming exceptional.

Cadence Questions

1. What exceptional person do you admire and wish you could emulate in your life and practice?

2. What are the habits and routines that they have in their business and life?

3. How could you mirror those in a way that would work in your own practice and life and help provide momentum towards building a world class brand?

Big Goals

If you're Australian (or even if you're not) you'll likely have heard of Turia Pitt. We spoke of her previously in this book. She is an ultra-marathon runner who was caught in a grass fire while running a race in the Australian desert. She suffered burns to 65% of her body, lost seven fingers, had over 200 medical procedures and spent two gruelling years in recovery.

---

71 Fogg, BJ. (2019). Tiny Habits: The Small Changes That Change Everything. HMH Books.

72 Fogg. Tiny Habits.

While she was in hospital, the doctors told her that she was probably never going to run ever again. But this wasn't an option for Turia. She loved to run. So she decided to set herself a goal. She decided that she was going to complete the Ironman once she had recovered.

Her then boyfriend Michael and her mother would come to see her in hospital every day to help her with her physiotherapy. They knew about her goal and they fully supported her. So every day they would say to her, 'Come on, let's start. It's time for your Ironman training.' And though it took her five years to achieve it, she did. That was Turia's big goal, and it was an achievement that was truly exceptional.

Big goals are a vital part of achieving momentum in our brands. Jim Collins talks about setting BHAGs, or big hairy audacious goals, in his book *Good to Great* he says, 'Even the highest performing organizations in the world have some kind of aspirational goal that helps pull them towards where they're trying to go.'[73] And we need to be doing the same. Setting goals that pull us towards our own exceptionality.

Joanne Love, who is an expert in high performance and a Paralympic coach for the Australian Paralympic swim team, has completed incredible research around setting not just goals, but healthy goals.[74] Her background is working with high-performance athletes, particularly swimmers, who are suffering mental health issues as a result of poor goal setting many years ago.

She says that you need to really set just three goals at a time, and they all need to be within your control. Two need to be achievable, and one needs to be aspirational. She said that specific balance is what creates

---

73 Collings, J. (2001). Good To Great. Century – Trade.
74 Love, J. (2021). Gold Medal Goals: The difference between goals that can help and goals that can harm. Proactive Performance Australia.

a result, and, therefore, the incredibly exceptional athletes that she works with. [75] She applies this same formula when she's working with businesses, organisations, leaders, teams and CEOs. I've included her goal-setting techniques in my own practice as well.

Having big goals, as long as they are well curated to be healthy and drive you towards results that are good for you and your brand, are an important part of building the momentum towards becoming world class.

Big Goals Questions

1. What are the most significant goals that you would like to achieve?

2. When would you like to achieve them?

Now it's time to set them no matter how crazy they may seem.

Create Every Day

Exceptional people are focused people and in order to become exceptional (and continue being exceptional) they focus on continuous improvement consistently. But what do they do to continuously improve? Well one thing they do is find a way to create every day.

Exceptional people don't just magically appear, or become exceptional overnight. They are made by their continuous drive towards exceptionality which they undertake every day (and continue to do so today). Creating every day is part of the process that helps them to become world class.

---

75 Love. Gold Medal Goals.

Exceptional people are focused people and in order to become exceptional (and continue being exceptional) they focus on continuous improvement consistently.

When you are creating every day – whether that's writing articles, working through podcasts, delivering on stage or online, writing books or something else entirely – it's a little bit like turning on a tap. If you haven't got the tap turned on, nothing's going to come out. So, you've got to actually turn the tap on to make sure that the creativity can come out and find space to grow. Exceptional people turn that tap on every day.

Albert Einstein said, 'Creativity is seeing what others see and thinking what no one else has ever thought.' Creating is your space for letting that creativity – that thought leadership – take wings and become something more.

Ken Done is one of my favourite artists. I grew up in the 80s and all my friends had beautiful, bright-coloured bedspreads based off of his distinctive and unique art. From then until today, he's been an inspiration to me. In fact, he's probably the reason why I wear a lot of colour, because it always feels bright, fun and joyful and reminds me of his work.

Ken Done is a fantastic example of someone who works towards becoming exceptional. You can look back to the 80s and see how his work has evolved and continues to evolve today. And that's because he still creates every day. He's continuing to get better all the time.

Mykel Dixon, who wrote the book, *Everyday Creative,* talks about how being able to unpack and create every day means that you become more innovative.[76] His research shows that you actually become more progressive[77] and eventually, in my opinion, world class. But how do you achieve this? How do you make time and space?

---

76 Dixon, M. (2020). Everyday Creative: A Dangerous Guide for Making Magic at Work. Wiley.

77 Dixon. Everyday Creative.

Begin small. First, simply block time to focus on your thing. It might only be five minutes if that's all you can spare at the moment. For me, it's a short 10 minutes a day. But during those 10 minutes I write out my thoughts and ideas. I capture them in a document, and I may use them in a blog, or in the chapter of a book or even in my socials or podcast. But regardless, I've captured them in that moment so I can use them. Even better, the act of creating leads to more time and energy for creating because you've built up the cadence for that practice in your own business.

Create Everyday Questions

1. What do you do every single day that helps you move towards becoming world class? If there's nothing yet, then ask yourself...

   a. What's your 'thing'?

   b. How can you block time every single day to do that?

Make Mistakes

Make no mistake, exceptional people do (make mistakes). And while no one enjoys the process of slipping up, exceptional people understand that it's part of their progress and that they are the rule, as opposed to the exception. Most importantly, exceptional people aren't afraid of making mistakes. This makes them better at taking risks and taking on the necessary challenges and goals that can help them grow into exceptional people and create a world class brand.

On the other hand, when we're afraid of making mistakes we can lose confidence in our own abilities. We accelerate less and take on fewer risks generally. And any mistakes that we do make have the power to completely derail our forward progression. But in order to become exceptional and build a world class brand, we have to move past mistakes quickly and quietly, not dwell on them. Because they are the only way that you can make progress.

In fact research shows that while most of us try to get through life without making mistakes, this is actually counter-productive to real learning.[78] Because real learning occurs in the errors. Where errors are made, and then corrective feedback is taken, it's actually highly beneficial to learning. In fact, this is the method that leads to optimal performance.[79]

Carol Dweck's research identifies this approach as the growth mindset, and it's a vital part of becoming truly exceptional.[80] Carol, who is a Professor of Psychology at Stanford University, says, 'Individuals who believe their talents can be developed (through hard work, good strategies, and input from others) have a growth mindset. They tend to achieve more than those with a more fixed mindset (those who believe their talents are innate gifts). This is because they worry less about looking smart and they put more energy into learning.'[81]

When you have a growth mindset you aren't overwhelmed or taken down by mistakes. Instead, you are able to see that you've made a

---

78 Metcalfe, J. (2017). Learning from Errors. Annual Review of Psychology. Accessed at https://www.annualreviews.org/doi/10.1146/annurev-psych-010416-044022.

79 Metcalfe. Learning from Errors.

80 Dweck, C. (2019). The Choice to Make a Difference. Perspectives on Psychological Science. Accessed at https://journals.sagepub.com/doi/10.1177/1745691618804180.

81 Dweck. (2017). Mindset: Changing The Way You Think To Fulfil Your Potential. Robinson.

mistake, but understand that it's simply time, energy and hard work that will help you get from where you are (making mistakes) to where you currently want to be (having achieved the task or objective).

In a commencement speech to the 2008 Stanford University graduating class, Oprah Winfrey told a story of one of her own big failures.[82] In 2007 she founded a school for girls in South Africa. But that very first year, the school was rocked with scandal when a dorm matron was accused of sexually abusing students. Oprah took immediate action, travelling to South Africa personally to work towards resolving the crisis. But she openly admits that the mistakes happened because she was not paying attention to the things that mattered.

She said, 'I understand now the mistakes I made, because I had been paying attention to all of the wrong things. I'd built that school from the outside in, when what really mattered was the inside out.'[83]

Oprah can take great heart (as can we all) from the quote by the great basketball coach, John Wooden. He said, 'If you're not making mistakes, then you're not doing anything. I'm positive that a doer makes mistakes.'

Of course when you continue to make the same mistakes over and over it can feel like you're stuck in quicksand. However, when you realise that making mistakes is actually about progress, then it is far easier to dip into the growth mindset, move on from the mire and actually grow from the experience.

---

82 Winfrey, O. Speech at Stanford's Commencement Ceremony. 15 June 2008. Stanford Report. Accessed at https://news.stanford.edu/news/2008/june18/como-061808.html.

83 Winfrey. Speech at Stanford's Commencement Ceremony.

I teach the benefit of making mistakes in my own work. The clients I work with launch a new project every 90 days, and they are fully prepared to fail half of them. I learned this methodology from being part of – and on the faculty of – Thought Leaders Business School. Through my own launches, my own failures and my own mistakes I learned first hand that this is the only way to really make progress.

In my own practice I've had to make some educated guesses and think about whether they would work or not. And many of them did not. But ultimately, when they failed, I was able to manage my own expectations, understanding that every failure was one step closer to success and building a world class brand.

Importantly, when you're willing to press forward despite mistakes (or perhaps because of them) and when you're not afraid to meet challenges and take on new ideas because of fear of making a mistake, you build your own momentum. And that's required to become a world class brand and an exceptional leader.

Making Mistakes Questions

1. Are you already embracing failure as a normal part of progress?

2. If not, how can you start?

3. Do you have people around you who have either progressed past the mistakes you're currently making, or have made a lot of mistakes but are still successful? How can you learn from them to shortcut your own processes?

Consistency

Consistency is the last element that forms part of how we build momentum towards becoming world class. How does it work?

When we are consistent in our communications and actions, we build trust and confidence in our brand. This isn't just about having a consistent tone of voice, or logo and colour palette. This is about showing up rain, hail or shine for your audience, clients and customers. Yes, it takes effort, but over time, when you're consistent, people will be drawn to you. On the other hand, without consistency, people lose confidence and trust in you.

So the first question we need to ask ourselves in terms of consistency is what holds us back? For many of us the answer is going to be a lack of rhythm and cadence in our habits and routines which can help us become consistent in the activities that create exceptionality.

It's a little bit like losing weight. You might say, 'Oh, well, I've just got to eat less calories and exercise a bit more.' But unless you have it in the calendar every day, unless you have the reminders of what exactly you need to do and the systems and processes around that, then you'll lose that war every time.

In the same way, you need processes in place to support your exceptionality. Without that consistency you simply won't succeed. You'll lose trust, lose confidence and, therefore, lose the chance to build a world-class, exceptional brand. Dwayne Johnson, the American actor said, 'Success isn't always about greatness. It's about consistency. Consistent hard work leads to success. Greatness will come.'

Research supports the Rock's perspective. In fact one seminal study showed that groups became and remained effective as long as they did not change leaders.[84] On the other hand, when leadership changed, even where both leaders were equally effective, then effectiveness dropped.[85] This is because people trust consistent leaders.

One fantastic example of a consistent practice is Emily Varvra. She is a motivational speaker, presenter and sales expert, and she shows up every single day on social media with a motivational video sharing her expertise and inspiring her audience. She does an incredible job of making sure that she's really consistent in her engagement outreach, and connecting with her audience. And as a result she's also ranked as one of the top sales people in the world, particularly in direct selling space.

Consistency Questions

1. What is your vision or your goal for you as a leader and as a brand?

2. Who is your audience? Where are they hanging out? And how can you reach them consistently?

3. What are the rhythms, systems and cadences you need to put in place to support you to do that every single day, week, month and year?

---

84 Pryer, M, Flint, A and Bass, B. Group Effectiveness and Consistency in Leadership. December 1962. American Sociological Association. Accessed at https://www.jstor.org/stable/2785777.

85 Pryer. Group Effectiveness.

Conclusion

Building momentum in your practice is a combination of having cadence – systems and processes – that put you into flow, setting goals that can drive you along your journey, creating every day within your area of genius, making mistakes along the way that you can then learn and grow from and showing up consistently in your business.

But with this combination of elements you are able to move past the friction that slows down business growth and instead sail along your individual path of continuous improvements. And it's this path that leads to a world-class brand.

Chapter 10

World Class Motivation

Understanding your own motivation is important to becoming world class. If you don't understand *why* you want to strive towards excellence, you'll quickly lose the willpower to do that. But everybody will have their own unique motivators. And the things that drive me, may not be the things that drive you.

However, there are some things that all brands with world-class motivation will inevitably have in common.

Where Does Motivation Come From?

When going on a journey to becoming exceptional, we need to question how we source our motivation. Sometimes we can consider things like our purpose, but there are a lot of other things that can be used to really identify where motivation comes from, and to drive and create the fuel for that motivation.

When you have motivation, it's like a magnet pulling you. It feels like it's just something that you want to happen – or even that it's inevitable. It is *going* to happen. And in most cases, for exceptional people, this comes from inside of themselves.

Understanding your own motivation is important to becoming world class. If you don't understand why you want to strive towards excellence, you'll quickly lose the willpower to do that.

Richard Ryan and Edward Deci are the researchers behind the self-motivation theory.[86] Self-motivation suggests that people are motivated to grow and persevere by innate internal universal psychological needs, such as purpose and connection. And that these innate needs far outweigh any external validation they might otherwise receive.[87]

Participants in a study were asked to complete a puzzle. One group was paid for their time, while the other wasn't offered any remuneration or reward whatsoever. When the allotted time to complete the task was up, the group that were not being paid were more motivated to continue to solve the puzzle.[88] On the other hand, the group that was paid for their time, simply left when the time was up.[89] This is because they had no intrinsic motivation to solve the problem for themselves.

There are three key things that drive self-motivation.

1. The first is autonomy. Those who are self-motivated have a feeling of being the master of their own destiny and a sense of control over their outcomes.

2. The second is competence. This is a knowledge or a skill in terms of the ability to get things done within their area of expertise.

3. And the third is connectedness, which is essentially feeling like they relate to and can connect with the right people.

---

86 O'Hara, D. The intrinsic motivation of Richard Ryan and Edward Deci. 18 December 2017. American Psychological Association. Accessed at https://www.apa.org/members/content/intrinsic-motivation.

87 O'Hara. The intrinsic motivation.

88 Deci, E. Effects of Externally Mediated Rewards on Intrinsic Motivation. Journal of Personality and Social Psychology. 1971. Accessed at https://selfdeterminationtheory.org/SDT/documents/1971_Deci.pdf.

89 Deci. Effects of Externally Mediated Rewards.

This brings a sense of belonging and a close and affectionate relationship with those who are affected by their work.

Having self-motivation is a key part of becoming exceptional. After all, exceptionality is a level above and beyond what the average person is accomplishing. So there is no one out there to drive you – no one else is reaching for the same heights, or pushing you to accomplish the same. It is up to the exceptional individual to continue to push and strive for better and better outcomes in order to become exceptional and have a world-class brand.

Winston Churchill is often called the greatest statesman of the twentieth century. In fact, he led Britain through one of the worst crises of its history – World War II – off the back of his relentless passion and absolute belief in their ultimate success. He's described as someone who 'perpetually demonstrated enthusiasm, determination, and optimism'.[90] And this did not come from an external place, but was totally driven by his own self-motivation.

One of Churchill's private secretaries said this of Churchill after being elected Prime Minister:

'The effects of Churchill's zeal was [sic] felt immediately in Whitehall. Government departments which under Neville Chamberlain had continued to work at much the same speed as in peacetime awoke to the realities of war. A sense of urgency was created in the course of very few days and respectable civil servants were actually to be seen running along the corridors. No delays were condoned; telephone

---

90 Churchill: Leader and Statesman. International Churchill Society. Accessed at https://winstonchurchill.org/the-life-of-churchill/life/churchill-leader-and-statesman/#:~:text=Historians%20widely%20attribute%20Churchill%20with,passion%3B%20and%20his%20imperturbable%20personality.

switchboards quadrupled their efficiency; the Chiefs of Staff and the Joint Planning Staff were in almost constant session; regular office hours ceased to exist and weekends disappeared with them.'[91]

Churchill was internally motivated to make big changes in his work – and to raise all those around him to his own exceptional level as well. And he continued to make changes and improvements throughout his tenure in office because, as he said himself, 'Success is not final and failure is not fatal. It is the courage to continue that counts.'

Dr Louise Mahler is another example of someone who demonstrates incredible self-motivation. Louise is an expert in communication and exceptional at what she does. And when you listen to her and how she speaks and talks about her area of expertise, you can see just how self-motivated she is.

For Louise, this comes from the high sense of freedom and control she feels over her life. In other words, she chooses the clients that she wants to work with. She chooses what she wants to work on. She knows how to do what she wants to do, and she's written books on the topic. She knows exactly what she's doing, and she absolutely loves helping people to achieve the outcomes they are looking for.

When speaking with her, she constantly says, 'I just love what I do. I absolutely love it.' She's a great example of the self-determination theory at play. She is highly motivated. She has survived through difficult times in her business, and has largely managed her business by herself. Considering the growth in her business, it's quite extraordinary how much she's actually been capable of and her capacity to do the work.

---

91   Churchill: Leader and Statesman.

Motivation Questions

When you're looking at your own motivation to determine where it comes from, ask yourself these questions:

1. What is it that drives you?

2. Where do you feel like you have control in your career, in your business and in your life?

3. Where do you feel most competent?

4. What are the skills that you have, and how do these align with your uniqueness?

5. Finally, who is the beneficiary? Who's your customer? Who's the person who receives the outcomes as a result of the work that you do?

Motivation To Take Risks

Motivation is a benefit when you're building a world-class brand because it pushes you forward to try more, do more and be more. And in many cases this involves taking risks.

Amelia Earhart was the first female to fly across the Atlantic and also to fly around the world. She was brave, she was strong and she was a person who always thought out of the square box. Most importantly, Amelia had faith in herself, especially when it came to taking risks. She famously said, 'Decide whether or not the goal is worth the risks involved. And if it's not, stop worrying.'

When you're on the path to becoming exceptional, you need to take risks to do the things that you've never done before. Without risks, there is no progress, even if there is failure along the way. You have to become comfortable with discomfort and doing things you've never done before.

Jim Collins, in his book *Good to Great*, talks about firing bullets and cannonballs, and the small and big risks that you'll come across in your growth, particularly on your journey to exceptionality.[92] The key is getting the balance of those right so that you're consciously aware of what are bullets and what are cannonballs and how you cope with those along the way.

He says, 'First, you fire bullets (low-cost, low-risk, low-distraction experiments) to figure out what will work—calibrating your line of sight by taking small shots. Then, once you have empirical validation, you fire a cannonball (concentrating resources into a big bet) on the calibrated line of sight. Calibrated cannonballs correlate with outsized results; uncalibrated cannonballs correlate with disaster. The ability to turn small proven ideas (bullets) into huge hits (cannonballs) counts more than the sheer amount of pure innovation.'[93]

Once you've learned how to create the bullets and cannonballs – and how to take these risks – you'll need to understand what you need to do in order to create safety nets around that risk taking.

First, you'll need to build a strong network of diverse people around you with different perspectives, ideas and experiences. Second, you must practice being agile. You need to be able to change plans, take different approaches and appraise what's happening along the way. Third, you'll

---

92 Collins. Good To Great.

93 Collins, J. Fire Bullets, Then Cannonballs. Accessed at https://www.jimcollins.com/concepts/fire-bullets-then-cannonballs.html.

need to share your goals with people. When you share your goals, people will tend to buy in a bit more and provide more support. This both reduces your risk and also inspires people. And fourth and last, you need to stay focused on the people who matter, and more often than not, that's your customer. If you can remain customer centric, you're more likely to be able to weather the risks, and they will always remain intentional and outcome focused.

Hang Out With Those Who Shift Your Internal Dialogue

Exceptional people don't achieve a world-class practice on their own. Just as we've described above, they have to surround themselves with the right people, to help them to progress to becoming world class. If they don't, they'll fall into self-doubt, worry and fear, and they'll lose their sense of social proof. Creating a social norm around you builds up a sense of belonging and safety for you to take risks.

When you have the right people around you, it's kind of like having a life jacket on. You're about to go into choppy seas, or places and destinations that you've never been before, and yes, you could sink. When you have the right people around you, it increases your sense of safety. But it also increases your actual safety, in that you have a higher chance of success.

Robin Dunbar, the author of the book, *How Many Friends Does One Person Need?*, identified that successful people and leaders, and in this case, exceptional people, have an incredible network around them.[94] But there's also a system to it, which he refers to as Dunbar's numbers.[95]

---

94 Dunbar, R. (2010). How Many Friends Does One Person Need?: Dunbar's Number and Other Evolutionary Quirks. Harvard University Press.

95 Dunbar. How Many Friends.

With Dunbar's numbers, he identified that exceptional people have an inner circle around them of about five people. Then they have a slightly larger circle of 15, and then a big circle of 150 friends.[96] This helps them to engage and connect without spreading themselves too thin. It also serves the purpose of ensuring that they have a tight group around them that understands where they are and can have an influence on their success.

Matt Church, the founder of Thought Leaders Business School, says that we need to be inspired by the company we keep. And Jim Rohn, entrepreneur and motivational leader, says that we are the sum of the five people we hang out with most.[97] So we need to make sure that these people are those that are willing to support us as we take the risks necessary to become world-class and exceptional leaders.

A great example is Lady Gaga. If we look at her and her collaborations, for example, we can see that Lady Gaga is clearly on a mission to become an iconic Hollywood star, and somebody who will be remembered for generations. The people that she hangs out with are not just emerging or contemporary artists. She has collaborated with Tony Bennett and Beyoncé. She appeared on the stage at the Academy Awards with Liza Minnelli. She's very deliberate in who she associates herself with because she understands the brand that she's trying to build.

In the programs I run, for example, Women with Influence, I'm very deliberate about putting the participants into groups of 10 that will help

---

96 Dunbar. How Many Friends.

97 Groth, A. You're The Average Of The Five People You Spend The Most Time With, 25 July 2012. Business Insider. Accessed at https://www.businessinsider.com/jim-rohn-youre-the-average-of-the-five-people-you-spend-the-most-time-with-2012-7#:~:text=Motivational%20speaker%20Jim%20Rohn%20famously,the%20average%20of%20all%20outcomes.

them to feel that sense of 'life jacket' safety. With the community around them, they feel more confident in doing things they've never done before. We all need to be developing this safety net for ourselves as well.

Risk Questions

1. Specifically, who are in your five, 15 and 150 circle?

2. Have they achieved what you are trying to achieve? Do they inspire you?

3. Are they able to guide you and help you navigate through the choppy waters that you are navigating?

Motivation to Execute Excellence

In order to become world class and exceptional we have to execute everything we do with excellence. Of course, this begins by looking at our own personal brands and strengths – including how we relate to our customers and how we drive growth. If we don't consider our customers and just focus on ourselves, then we lose our exceptionality and relevance to our audience.

In the book, *The Discipline of Market Leaders*, authors Fred Wiersema and Michael Treacy identify exceptional organisations – those that are considered market leaders and the best in the world at what they do – and what makes them exceptional.[98]

---

98 Wiersema, F and Treacy, M. (1997). The Discipline of Market Leaders: Choose Your Customers, Narrow Your Focus, Dominate Your Market. Basic Books.

In their research they identified three specific traits that are in these exceptional organisations.

1. The first is operational excellence. That is around the systems, processes that an organisation has.

2. The second is customer intimacy. This is the level of connection the organisation has with their customers.

3. The third is product leadership, which is about innovation and creativity and being a leader in creating a really unique product.

These prongs act a little bit like a three-wheeled bike. Every organisation that is exceptional or a market leader has these traits, but one will have more weight in one area than in another. And true organisational excellence demands that you are better than yourself.

This is true for us in our practice areas as well. When you aspire to execute excellence and become exceptional, you have to keep looking at the current version of yourself and ask yourself, how do you want to continue? What are you going to do to keep being the very best and continue to strive to be world class?

Let's take a look at Apple. They have incredible product leadership and some customer intimacy. Amazon, on the other hand, excels in operational excellence and dips into customer intimacy. In both cases, they are a combination of the two elements.

So, when we're looking at our personal brand, or our brand as a leader, we need to determine what makes us exceptional and what we do best to elevate our excellence. Are we focused on systems and processes? Are we best at providing customer intimacy and building authentic relationships? Or do our real strengths lie in our products – or the way we provide programs and solutions for our customers or clients?

If you can work out what that is for you, your business and your brand, then not only are you going to be unique, but you're going to continue to develop excellence and relevance with your market.

Executing Excellence Questions

1. What are some examples of brands that you love?

2. Which aspects of these brands do you most relate to? Is it product leadership, operational excellence or customer intimacy?

3. Which model do you most aspire to in order to strive to achieve excellence?

Motivation to Find Your Vision and Purpose

Steve Jobs once said, 'If you're working on something exciting that you really care about, you don't have to be pushed. The vision pulls you.' I remember running a workshop for a group of CEOs. When I was working with them, one of the things that I asked them to do was to articulate to me their vision for their business? Many of them really struggled with being able to articulate what their vision was. Except for one person.

Nick Barnsdall, the CEO of Caterpillar Equipment, was the one exception. He told the entire group that he had taken over the CEO role because his business partner, the former CEO, had died in a car accident.

His death had a profound effect on Nick and it completely changed his vision for Caterpillar Equipment. He said, 'I'm not here just to run a business. I'm here to create, and to leave the legacy of this business that he and I went in together to do.' He said, 'This is what we wanted to do together. We wanted to have an impact for our customers. We wanted to create something extraordinary.' He added, 'I also need to ensure the security of his family.'

Nick was also quite young at the time, so he was having to liaise with the former CEO's family a lot, all while still trying to find his feet. It was a very stressful time for him. But he was on an absolute mission and his purpose was to get them through that time and be able to deliver.

Out of all the CEOs that I worked with that year, and I worked with hundreds of them, he was the only one who was able to truly articulate his vision and mission. He is now the owner of at least 13 companies and is well and truly on track to do over $150 million in revenue. He's also written two books, has his own podcast and has continued to hone his craft around educating small business owners to help them to grow their businesses and manage their own risk. And I'm lucky enough to continue to work with him today.

When you have your purpose and your vision, you feel like you have a lighthouse – a guiding light that can help you. Even when you're tired, struggling or failing, your purpose and vision creates a beacon for you, and for your customers and audience to connect with. And like a lighthouse it keeps shining the light on the way forward. How you get there may change, but at least the beacon is showing you where to go.

Simon Sinek, wrote the book, *Start With Why*. In it he identifies that great brands and great leaders have a sense of purpose, meaning and connection.[99] They understand why they're doing what they're doing, why it matters and the impact it could have on their audience and community. And this is what you need to do in your own work. Identify your own why. Why are you doing what you do? And – most importantly – why does it matter?

This is the final and most important step to giving you the motivation you need to continue along the path to building a world-class brand and continually striving for exceptionality.

Motivation Questions

1. What are you trying to become most known for?

2. What is your lighthouse?

3. What is your purpose?

4. What is the vision that you are trying to create?

Conclusion

Being a world-class practice is an essential part of becoming exceptional. And when you understand the power of exceptionality and how to identify your own uniqueness, the world-class practice becomes the final prong that supports you on your path to becoming exceptional.

---

99 Sinek, S. (2011). Start with Why: How Great Leaders Inspire Everyone to Take Action. Portfolio.

In Closing

This book covers a lot of ground from having an exceptionality mindset to defining your uniqueness and committing to becoming world class, and all of it centers on the act of finding your own powerful positioning. The concepts in the book are designed to start the conversation and inspire you rather than make you feel overwhelmed. They're designed to help you consider how they may apply for you, your team and organisation as well as to help you consider what builds your brand, and your trust, connection and influence with the people who matter in your world.

The ideas behind this book are designed to help give you a framework to consider, measure and gain insights into the areas where you have strengths and into other areas where you might have an opportunity to focus on and improve. As each area improves there is a continuous levelling up that occurs whether it's each day, quarter or year as you make more conscious and intentional choices around trust in building your tribe.

The key to remember is not to be afraid to start small. Whilst learning to put yourself out there may seem like a huge mountain to climb, it starts with you taking a small step. One conversation, one idea at a time. Take the lead and be the example that others can follow. From there the ripple of change begins that will ultimately lead you to become closer and closer to exceptional every single day.

I would love to hear how you go implementing these strategies and striving towards exceptionality. Please reach out to share your stories and examples to me at jane@jane-anderson.com.au.

I'm cheering you on!

The key to remember is not to be afraid to start small. Whilst learning to put yourself out there may seem like a huge mountain to climb, it starts with you taking a small step. One conversation, one idea at a time. Take the lead and be the example that others can follow. From there the ripple of change begins that will ultimately lead you to become closer and closer to exceptional every single day.

Work With Jane

In a world of constant change, there is a greater need for consultants and experts in their fields to lead and help their clients navigate change. To do this they need a highly influential personal brand, catalyst content and effective business support to build their tribe.

With over 25 years experience, Jane has been named as one of the top three branding experts in the world. She has helped over 150,000 people to build their identity and influence. She is a certified speaker, coach and has been featured on *Sky Business*, *The Today Show*, *The Age*, *Sydney Morning Herald*, *BBC* and *Management Today*. The author of 10 books, including *Exceptionality*, Jane typically speaks at conferences, runs workshops, consults and coaches. She also has a particular focus on female leaders helping them to build their personal brands, thought leadership and sales.

Jane holds one of the top 1% viewed LinkedIn profiles and is the host of the *Jane Anderson Show* Podcast where she has interviewed modern thinkers such as Seth Godin.

She has also won over 24 marketing, business and coaching industry awards.

CORPORATE CLIENTS HAVE INCLUDED:

Telstra, International Rice Research Institute, Wesfarmers, Amadeus, Virgin Australia, IKEA, LEGO, Mercedes-Benz, Australian Medical Association, Shell Energy and Workcover.

Book in a time to chat here:

https://calendly.com/jane-0877/complimentary-discussion
or email Jane's team at support@jane-anderson.com.au or call the
office at +61 7 3841 7772.

Alternatively jump on Jane's website at www.jane-anderson.com.au to find out about her workshops, speaking and coaching programs.

Read More of Jane's Work

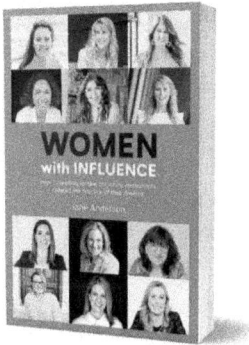

With more than 60% of small businesses in Australia started by women, and many women not returning to work post COVID-19, the opportunity for female experts to run their own consulting practices has become more popular than ever.

This book shares the journey of 12 women who started their consulting practices selling to organisations. These interviews share the excitement, challenges, disappointments and aspirations to do work that is fulfilling, fun and creates the freedom that they all have craved.

Be inspired by these women who are leading the way in the future of work!

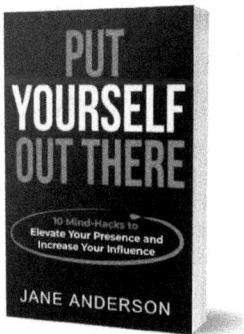

There used to be a saying that 'good things come to those who wait', but times have changed. There is now a level playing field. It's time to step up, stand out and put yourself out there.

With the pace of change means it's impossible to keep up to date with algorithms and the platform technology. What's really going on is the fear of being judged, the imposter syndrome, the fear of rejection and the fear of failure.

Whether you want to work with dream clients, ask someone on a date, apply for that job, share your ideas or create a social following, Jane shares the top 10 mind hacks that she has used with thousands of clients to help them find the courage to put themselves out there, and how you can apply them too.

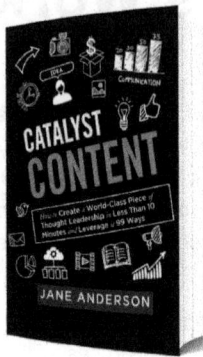

The content marketing market share is expected to increase by USD 487.24 billion from 2021 to 2026, a massive increase from just USD 156 billion in 2015.

The rate of growth in content consumption has been dramatic and the risk is that we start to create noise over signals.

In this book Jane talks about the power of thought leadership and how to put your ideas out there. She discusses the concepts of becoming prolific by creating the cadence of catalyst content that drives change.

This book is ideal for thought leaders, content creators and consultants looking to improve the quality and consistency of their thought leadership and content creation.

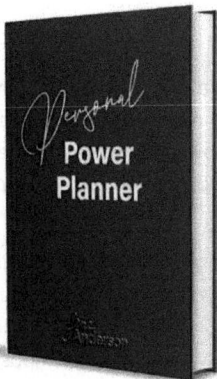

Did you know you're 40% more likely to achieve your goals if you write them down? That research led me to custom design this Personal Power Planner which can help you stay aligned with your plan every day.

Premium quality 100-page daily planner.

Designed to help you focus and stay aligned with your vision and goals – every day.

Simple, effective approach to managing time so you get your work done.

Includes a video guide on how to use your personal power planner to elevate your time management and achieve your goals.

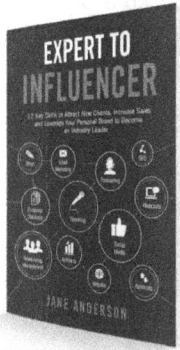

The old ways of growing a business have changed.

Social media has levelled the playing field and now it's easier than ever to compete with the big players in your industry.

Whether you're a thought leader, a trusted advisor, an academic or an expert, the way you position and market yourself is now more important than ever.

This book will help you uncover the 12 secret activities to grow your business and opportunities.

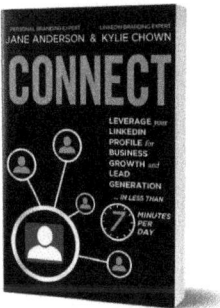

Never has there been an opportunity for businesses and consultants to identify, engage and connect with their ideal audience like there is now with LinkedIn.

By the end of this book, you will have the strategies you need to generate leads and grow your business using LinkedIn. You will be armed with practical steps that you can implement straight away to see real results. Your outcomes will be stronger, and you will lead the competition on this new playing field.

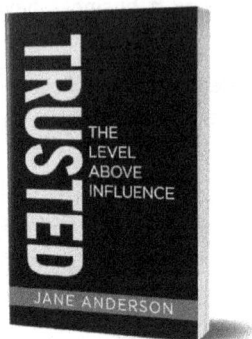

In a world of disruption and constant change, we've become more transparent than ever.

Organisations and their leaders at all levels are challenged with adapting to changing customer demands, leading growth and attracting and retaining great talent. They're being asked to be more transparent, authentic and credible than ever.

In this sea of noise and trying to make sense of so much change, customers and employees connect with those who they trust.

In this book, Jane covers the nine key skills of high-trust brands and global influencers that lead with influence and communicate during change.

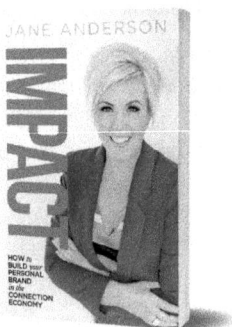

We're no longer in the industrial or information age. We're now in the connection economy, where your ability to stand out, connect with others and position yourself in your career and business means security. It means you won't be left behind but instead be ahead of the pack.

Companies and governments no longer want people who want jobs for life. They want innovation, ideas and networks to thrive in volatile economic times. We are bombarded with information and choices every day. Hard work alone doesn't cut it anymore.

Discover how to create 'corporation you' without being a tall poppy to build your personal brand.

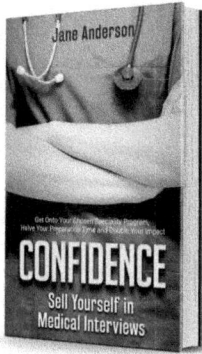

We all hate selling ourselves, but interviews are one of those times when you can't be shy. You have to stand out from the crowd. There's a way to give the panel what they want to hear without sounding like you're blowing your own trumpet.

From this book, you will learn techniques to increase your confidence, how to anticipate the questions the panel might ask and how to practice in the lead-up to the big day.